Project Kindness

What does the Lord require of you: but to do justice,
love kindness and walk humbly with your God.
Micah 6.8

Project Kindness

Faith and hope in contested times

Ellen Loudon

First published in 2026 by the Canterbury Press Norwich

Editorial office
3rd Floor, Invicta House
110 Golden Lane
London EC1Y 0TG, UK
www.canterburypress.co.uk

Canterbury Press is an imprint of Hymns Ancient & Modern Ltd
(a registered charity)

Hymns Ancient & Modern

Hymns Ancient & Modern® is a registered trademark of
Hymns Ancient & Modern Ltd
13A Hellesdon Park Road, Norwich,
Norfolk NR6 5DR, UK

British Library Cataloguing in Publication data

A catalogue record for this book is available
from the British Library

ISBN: 978 1 78622 740 9

EU GPSR Authorised Representative
LOGOS EUROPE, 9 rue Nicolas Poussin, 17000, LA ROCHELLE, France
E-mail: Contact@logoseurope.eu

Typeset by Regent Typesetting

Contents

This book is dedicated to Mark Loudon

I am grateful to family, friends and colleagues who have been so very kind. Particularly Andrea, Barry, Eleanor, Elise, Eva, Joe, John D, Kev, Richard P and the Loudon family; and to my doggo companions, who are the kindest of creatures: Jacob, Holly and Mr Tig.

Love is patient; love is kind; love is not envious or boastful or arrogant or rude. It does not insist on its own way; it is not irritable; it keeps no record of wrongs; it does not rejoice in wrongdoing but rejoices in the truth. It bears all things, believes all things, hopes all things, endures all things. Love never ends.

1 Corinthians 13.4–8a

Foreword

Jane was my primary school friend who has always stood out in my memory as someone who was kind. It is a long time since those days, yet the essence of her kindness remains with me. Was it that I don't ever remember falling out with her? Or is it that she embodied something of the fruit of the Spirit that St Paul speaks of in Galatians 5.22–23?

I doubt that as children there were not moments of disagreement, yet somehow I was never left with a feeling of hurt. In this world where there seems a growing sense of anxiety and fear, and fracture permeates our society and personal relationships, kindness is something that stands out as a mark of grace.

Acts of kindness by strangers are heralded as an unusual gift of generosity. I remember with gratitude the man whose name I never knew, whom I met at the bus stop on my way to school most days, who gave me his umbrella in torrential rain. I recall the woman who paid our restaurant bill anonymously having recognized me as the priest who had prayed with her once. And then there are the friends who have gone the extra mile to show their care.

In this book Ellen draws on personal conversations with a wide range of contributors, and reflects on how kindness impacts our lives. She movingly shares her own story and muses on how kindness helps us to value past experience, live through present circumstance, and shapes our future.

In the Liverpool Diocese, where Ellen and I both serve as ministers within the Church, we are discovering more of how we can allow the Spirit of God to transform who we are as his people. Together Liverpool is a charity that works to create a fairer, kinder world through the Network of Kindness, and their work is featured in these pages. Stories of hope and inspiration are told on their website which bring to life something of what characterizes kindness.

Recent experience within the Church at large and locally across the diocese has caused us to be more intentional in wanting to develop a culture that can be identified as kind. One that brings us together through the inclusion and valuing of every single person and offers a safe space for each to flourish.

To that end we have been 'dwelling' in the verses from Colossians 3.12–17, which speak of how God sees us, and how, as we recognize our identity in Christ, we are called to grow a community of love and compassion that speaks of human kindness.

> Therefore, as God's chosen ones, holy and beloved, clothe yourselves with compassion, kindness, humility, meekness, and patience. Bear with one another and, if anyone has a complaint against another, forgive each other; just as the Lord has forgiven you, so you also must forgive. Above all, clothe yourselves with love, which binds everything together in perfect harmony. And let the peace of Christ rule in your hearts, to which indeed you were called in one body. And be thankful. Let the word of Christ dwell in you richly; teach and admonish one another in all wisdom; and with gratitude in your hearts sing psalms, hymns, and spiritual songs to God. And whatever you do, in word or deed, do everything in the name of the Lord Jesus, giving thanks to God the Father through him.

Ellen shares how kindness has brought a measure of healing in her own personal life, and we are beginning to find it so in the life of a diocese that has known hurt, anger and disappointment. I hope that as you read this book you too will find your life challenged and changed through the encountering of kindness and that it might encourage you to open yourself to its expression.

The Rt Revd Ruth Worsley
Interim Bishop of Liverpool, February 2026

Introduction

Try a little kindness[1]

This is a book about how people remain kind and continue to do justice even when things get hard. Some of these people are facing personal struggles – health challenges, social exclusion, profound grief, burn-out, etc. Others are wrestling with social, spiritual or cultural issues in the public eye, and they dig deep to remain merciful under the pressure of public scrutiny. Most of the people you will encounter in these pages are just ordinary kind people who are getting on with life and seeking the common good. I am a Christian, so I want to tell of the good news of the kingdom of God at work in the world today. Many of the people whose stories are told in this book are leaning into their faith – sometimes holding on to faith by their fingertips. Nearly all are Christians, but you'll also hear from a Jewish rabbi and a Muslim as well as people who don't profess a faith but hold on to kindness as a value. These are brave people for whom kindness has become something far more than simply being nice – these people have built their lives around ethical struggle for justice and mercy.

If you are looking for a straightforward definition or a history of kindness, then you won't find it in this book. If you need this then I can recommend *On Kindness* by Philips and Taylor[2] as the shortest and most comprehensive I have read, and for current academic thinking on kindness the Sussex Centre for Research on Kindness[3] is a useful resource. What you will find in this book is hope, and a lot of ideas of what kindness is about: how it can be defined, what it feels like, what it smells like, what colour it is, if God is kind, different words for kindness, how kindness relates to justice, how kindness helps us relate to each other and the world, how kindness can be used to seek the common good, and many other ideas that the contributors wrestle with during our conversations.

This book is also about the importance of kindness in my life. I thought I knew myself reasonably well – wife, mother, priest, social justice activist, private poet, academic, musician, performer, friend, dog lover – and I also thought I was reasonably kind. Then my world started to fracture in late 2019 when my husband Mark was diagnosed with cancer and in

2020 the world was thrown into a series of Covid pandemic lockdowns. I carried on working online while caring for my husband, walking the dogs, keeping the home fire burning by baking, whittling (my new and, as it turned out, too dangerous lockdown hobby) and drinking too much white wine.[4] Like many others, I gained weight and lost connection with myself and other people: being locked in the house with a dying man was hard. Hard for me, but so much harder for Mark – he was dying and there was nothing I could do to stop it. The palliative care team did their best to make him comfortable. But he was in a lot of pain, he struggled to eat and drink, and for the last few months of his life he rarely left the bed we had set up for him in the dining room of our clergy house.

One day, before Mark became bedbound and less able to speak, we were watching TV. We had had an argument (not very unusual – we loved a good bicker). We sat in grumpy silence for a while; and then I started chitter-chattering away about the pop music we were watching (it was a Friday night, and endless repeats of *Top of the Pops* were on BBC4). In the moment I'd forgotten he was sick. I turned my head; he was sitting on His Chair. He looked so small – like a Lowry matchstick man, pale and bony. At first my brain didn't compute that person as my Mark and then it did, and I started to cry uncontrollably. I am not sure I had shown much emotion until this moment – I was being stoic and strong – and besides, Mark was the person dying, not me. The argument was long forgotten, he called me over to him and in his Northern Irish lilt, he said:

> Ellen, I know this is so hard for you. Much harder for you than me. Soon I will be dead, one day I will go to sleep and won't wake up. That is easy. But then you will have to go on living. That will be harder. I am so sorry.

I sobbed and sobbed and hugged his bony body. I think that was the saddest and kindest thing anyone has ever said to me.

Mark died on 2 March 2021. He wasn't alone. It was a brutal and traumatic death. He died and we had to go on living.

We were still in a lockdown at the time of his funeral so only 30 people could attend – 30 people in Liverpool Cathedral, a building that could have seated over 1,500. Hundreds of people joined online, and many stood safely distanced outside the cathedral. We had a small family wake, then restrictions meant we had to return to our bubbles. I went back to work five weeks later. My friends Andrea and Barry moved in to keep an eye out for me. My daughter Eva went back to university; the other children went back to their families. We went on living.

The first year was cruel, the second year brutal (worse than the first), the third year my grief was no less intense and by then my physical health had deteriorated. My mobility was worsening, and I discovered that I'd had a stroke but had no idea when. I had just bumbled through a medical crisis blissfully unaware. Work had become increasingly stressful – senior leaders had left suddenly, the diocese was facing financial crisis, significant working relationships were strained, and the national Church seemed in freefall. I felt that I hardly knew myself any more.

During all this sadness and anxiety, kindness got me through. When some people were being inexplicably mean and cold, most were consistently kind. I never felt abandoned – even when I was poorly. People brought me supplies, called me, took me out, picked me up for hospital appointments, walked the dog, made me Sunday dinner, prayed for me, helped me with my work, cut me slack and urged me on. I gradually got a bit better and at the end of 2025 I was well enough to begin three months of study leave. Which is where I am now, writing this book in the beautiful retreat space at Sheldon in Devon.[5]

Mark and all those kind people are the inspiration for this piece of work. My experience of being shown immense kindness is transforming my grief and despair. Kindness doesn't make it go away but it is making it possible to bear. Kindness has become very important to me. I want to learn how to practise it, how to share it and how to make it happen. This is what Project Kindness is all about. So, to begin my kindness adventure I decided to talk to as many people as possible to find out what made them kind, what inspired them and why they thought kindness was important. I also wanted to hear about why people thought kindness isn't valued as primary in terms of being socially, culturally and politically transformative. Why don't we value goodness as highly as we do the production of goods? Why are we more interested in people's net value than we are their generosity? Why do we want to be well known for being successful and powerful instead of being noted for our kindness and compassion?

Many of the people I have spoken to as part of this project are friends; some are mentors and other people I have admired for their kindness. There are others who I didn't know until our conversation, but their names were suggested to me as kind people. I contacted about 100 people as part of the project, and you will meet about 60 in these pages. Not everyone I asked could contribute: some felt their contribution would be disingenuous because they were too broken to be kind; a few just couldn't fit it into their schedule; only a handful didn't get back to me. As you will see, the response was overwhelmingly positive. Everyone who took part is represented in some way. Each chapter is a short vignette, just a glimpse of the hour-long Zoom-call kindness conversation. I've tried to capture something unique offered by each contributor. The conversations are set out as a journal entry and structured in date order; I have included largely unedited quotations from each person and added some commentary of my own. The last chapter concludes these conversations with a reflection on emerging themes and potential next steps for what I have started to refer to as Project Kindness.

Every kindness conversation has been healing, every person has been overwhelmingly kind, the insights have inspired me to walk into a kinder future. This book tracks a path towards what I pray is an emerging kindness movement. Kindness has the potential to change lives for the better, to influence the way we interact with each other, how we model social justice, shape the political landscape, seek the common good and live as the people of God in community. There is an infectious quality to kindness that comes out through the pages of this book. My hope is that you are inspired by these kindness conversations and want to add your voice to an uprising of kindness in your context.

I

Hungry ghosts

Jonathan Swales, pioneer priest and poet

1 August 2025

East of Eden: Liverpool

She limps up Brownlow Hill
collar loose,
black shirt now greying –
bearing the weight of thirty years
spent wrestling with grace.
She was in the first wave –
back when a woman
at the altar
felt like a whispered rebellion.
In a vicarage too big,
its walls biting cold in winter –
though at least there's CCTV.
A mile or so from the city,
surrounded by shuttered shops,
smiles missing teeth,
and the low hum of sirens
that never quite fade away.
House for duty –
though most days it can feel
like exile wrapped in loyalty.
She pours tea at Chapter,
nods politely while someone fresh
from theological college
quotes Bonhoeffer or Barth
between bites of focaccia.
She wants to say,
'Try a week in Kensington,

then we'll talk discipleship.'
This Priest
passes Lime Street,
where a busker belts out
'Let It Be'
a voice weathered
but surprisingly in tune.
She slips a quid in his case,
murmurs a blessing neither believes
will change much –
but speaks it anyway.
By Bold Street,
she talks with a working girl
in leopard-print tights,
a smile like stone –
hard,
sharp,
kind.
They talk footie.
The Reds were playing last night
Then faith.
'You're sound, Rev,' she says.
She laughs as her friend lights a cig,
must've been a payday,
if not it's rollies or dimps.
Sometimes ministry smells
of cheap perfume,
tobacco,
and second chances,
third chances,
and many more.
She visits a refugee family
in Toxteth –
carrying a bag from the foodbank
and colouring books,
listening to a father
tell his story in broken English,
unbroken sorrow.
She loves this city –
loves the people,
likes most of them,

the grit and the grin,
the two cathedrals:
the big stone lad on the hill,
and Paddy's Wigwam –
spiky and strange,
like a prayer that never quite settled.
She's always called it that –
everyone used to.
But now she wonders:
can she still say that?
Or is it the kind of thing
you quietly retire?
This priest aint woke –
not in the tick tock
and twitter sense.
She's from the school
of bruised compassion,
where mercy is earned
in messy rooms,
not performed online.
The Liver Building looms –
a cathedral of capitalism,
history and empire,
stone birds staring seaward,
wings frozen in time.
She wonders what they've seen,
and what they're still waiting for.
She imagines them as Wild Geese,
Spirit brooding and
watching the city of Scouse.
This Priest gave her youth to the Church –
Sunday school with flannelgraph,
wrote sermons on borrowed typewriters,
baptised babies
who now bury their own.
What's left?
A leaking roof.
A pension that doesn't stretch.
Still,
each Sunday,
she stands in a draughty nave

with fifteen faithful,
and a broken sound system.
Believe it or not,
there's still an overhead projector
in the corner –
no money for the fancy kit
they have at the resource church.
Doesn't matter.
It really is okay.
Her ministry isn't planting.
It isn't even growth,
in the numbers sense.
It's to stay –
to offer palliative care
to a dying church –
so they die well,
in the faith,
in this parish.
She lifts the bread
like it matters.
Like he still shows up.
Like this –
this tired giving –
isn't for nothing.
And when she says,
'This is my body, broken for you,'
she means it.
Every syllable.
Every crack in her voice.
Every part of her
still believing,
mostly,
in a Kingdom
just
round
the corner.

Jon Swales[1]

Jon and I were together at the theological Trinity College, Bristol 20 years ago.[2] I have followed his ministry with a quiet admiration over the years. He has been in Leeds since 2007, and is now a mission priest at Lighthouse West Yorkshire,[3] described by Jon as 'a community for those battered and bruised by the storms of life'. Jon is the first person I speak to as I begin to gather this collection of kindness voices, and his gentle optimism sets the tone for the conversations ahead. Our time together is wonderful, full of joy and hope – but also full of realism about the cost of loving-kindness in a world of shadow and fear.

Jon describes his Lighthouse community as 'hungry ghosts: shadows of how God has called them to be'. This Christian community creates space for those who are ordinarily outsiders and left behind. His description of the welcome offered to street people and addicts reminds me of the Great Banquet (Luke 14.12–24) where the rich don't want to attend so the master sends out servants, saying:

> 'Quickly, get out into the city streets and alleys. Collect all who look like they need a square meal, all the misfits and homeless and down-and-out you can lay your hands on, and bring them here.' (*The Message*)

It is in this extension of hospitality that kindness is evident. Jon describes this as 'cruciform adaptation', the 'embodiment of kindness – kindness that has teeth'! Lighthouse is a place that takes safeguarding seriously and where kindness is formed ethically with a sensitivity that ensures continuity and longevity. Lighthouse doesn't shy away from love language – it places a high value on love and kindness even in the most challenging of situations. Jon's ministry and that of the community he inhabits is testament to what he describes as the 'slow burn miracle of love'. He tells me that miracles do happen in an instant – he is witness to such transformations of people who lay down lives of addiction as they step into faith. But mostly this is hard, truth-telling loving-kindness that is vulnerable and can be heart-breaking. I hear the heaviness in the way Jon speaks of the high mortality rates, untimely early deaths of friends by suicide, the sadness of watching people break under the weight of addiction. Even when necessary personal and professional boundaries are in place, maintaining a ministry of 'prophetic encouragement' is not easy. It requires the discipline of truth-telling and robust accountability.

Jon is inspiring, and his energy for this work is evident, but I know this comes at a cost. There have been times when balancing this prophetic work alongside family life has been hard. Also, he has fought hard to remain mainstream and connected to the diocese. Jon is a creative person (the poem above is testament to his creativity) who thrives on intellectual debate, and he loves talking about Jesus. Indeed, his Christological focus is evident throughout our conversation as he constantly refers to the Gospels. He insists that 'the best discipleship course is the Gospels', and that 'Jesus is the litmus test for kindness'.

As our conversation ends we reflect on the ordinary nature of kindness, how it is a type of wisdom that can't be legislated or manufactured. Receiving kindness slows things down, it connects people, is humbling and healing. 'We should never miss an opportunity to be kind,' muses Jon.

That is the grace-filled truth about kindness – it is an opportunity to connect and be connected. In the next few months, I will go on to speak to many other people about kindness but in this, my first kindness conversation with an old friend, I get a glimpse of the kingdom party where the guests are welcomed without judgement with loving-kindness.

2

Spiritual independence

David Hayward (aka The NakedPastor), artist, writer and pastor

4 August 2025

> An evolving faith brings new ideas and ancient paths together. It's about rebuilding and reimagining a faith that works not only for ourselves but for the whole messy, wide, beautiful world ... An evolving faith is a resilient and stubborn form of faithfulness that is well acquainted with the presence of God in the loneliest places and deepest questions.
>
> *Sarah Bessey*[1]

I have an original NakedPastor drawing – it's the one where the disciples are standing next to Mary and the other women after the resurrection. The 12 male disciples say: 'So, ladies, thanks for being the first to witness and report the Resurrection and we will take it from here.'[2] It hangs in a place of importance and is my daily reminder of the reality of the patriarchy, and it amuses me that a man has mansplained (or is that man-drawn) it for me. So, one of the first things I say to David is, 'I have one of your drawings.' This is a fangirl start to our kindness conversation.

David lives on the east coast of Canada with his wife Lisa. We are meeting online at 6.30 a.m. eastern time and David is sitting in a corner of a white room on a green chair, a painting behind him. He is relaxed and happy to chat about his 'naked, transparent' ministry. His ministry is as an artist, writer and pastor of The Lasting Supper online community.[3] This ministry enables people he encounters to find their 'spiritual independence' – a calling that emerged from his own faith journey and what he describes as 'deconstruction'.[4]

David began publicly asking questions about his faith on his blog in 2005 and one by one these questions started to unravel his way of knowing God and the Church. The questions broke down his previously accepted constructed systems and brought about fear and longing. The more he asked, the deeper the dislocation from his traditional faith community and, eventually, in 2010 he left formal church ministry. As a result, he lost his job as a pastor, his home, his Christian community and the security of the organization he had grown up in. This was not an easy journey, but he speaks as a man who is prepared to ask questions and is unafraid of the answers (or the potential of there not being answers!). For David, there has been a kindness in this re-evaluation of his faith. It hasn't been a solo self-indulgent endeavour. It has been about community and connectedness. This kindness is inclusive and starts with a vision for unity. 'Kindness is about the assumption,' he tells me, that

> we are all connected at a deep and fundamental level, that we're one. And then we work to make that happen, like we work to make that manifest around us in our world. But, if you approach the world-divisively, if you think there's people who are in and people who are out, people who are evil, people who are righteous, and people who belong and people who don't, then you're that division – you're going to make that manifest in your world. So I believe kindness has to be the fruit of that assumption that we are one. Scriptures intimate that there is now no dividing wall between us, Christ through the cross has broken down all barriers and that the All in All dwells in all and is the Father of us all ... that kind of language assumes a kind of a unity. There's no dividing wall between us.

This is a particular sense of unity: it pictures each of us growing into our 'spiritual independence' from faith systems as we grow in faith as individual children of God, loved uniquely but identified collectively as community. It suggests that these systems serve an important purpose in forming and holding fledgling faith. For some of us they remain the place for growth and freedom, but for others leaving these systems becomes vital to spreading wings, flourishing and flying. We are not all the same, our needs are different, and that's what makes us unique. 'Diversity is what's most beautiful,' David insists, 'and homogeneity to me is ... ruthlessly deadly. Kindness makes space for diversity.'

David dwells on the kindness of diversity and the uniqueness of each person in the eyes of a loving God who desires us to be human and not to strive for Godlike power. He tells me:

> I don't believe the Tower of Babel was an actual historical event. I think it's a myth that was developed to explain why are there so many frigging languages in the world, and why are there so many different peoples? And the explanation was, well, if we were all the same that would be hubris and dangerous. Maybe some biblical interpretations might mean it divides our power, and then we can't take over everything or become God. But it's also a reflection of just the beautiful diversity of the human race, and that's where peace can be. Peace is not achieved through conformity. It's achieved through agreement, mutual respect.

David frames kindness as unity in diversity and mutual respect. This is a vision of a community of independent thinking believers who in their questioning learn more about God and what it means to be human.

I ask about how kindness and justice mingle. There is a short thoughtful pause before David replies: 'Justice is not a feeling. Justice is not a hope or a thought or an intention. It's a do. It disrupts politeness.' He continues:

> One of the flashes of insight I have had in my life was when I realized that love is indiscriminate ... it's not Hollywood. It's not sentimental. It can be, but that's not the route. And even when Jesus is quoted to have said that justice is like the sun that shines on everyone, or the rain that falls on everyone. He didn't know about gravity at the time, but gravity pulls everyone. It's just that indiscriminate. And I think that's what the sower and the seed story is about. The root of that story is that, look at the sower. He casts a seed, and it goes everywhere. I think that's love. It falls on fertile soil, it falls on rock, it falls on the path, it falls into the weeds, it falls, the birds eat it – it's that indiscriminate casting – that is love. And if we can capture and understand love like that then when we get up in the morning with that, with that basic understanding of this indiscriminate love, it would flow through our lives. Practically with people we meet, and it would be indiscriminate.

David contends that religious leaders should fight back against conformity with beauty and creativity – to help people to be human, to be themselves in relation to a creator God who knows and loves them uniquely. He argues that we need to insist on person-centred systems that promote love and connectedness. That the Church can be courageous, be unafraid of chaos and the outsider voices. He implores us: 'Be present, warm, openhearted and adventurous.'

I love this vision for a universal church of glorious, fearless, indiscriminate love.

3

What will you risk for kindness?

Adjoa Andoh, actor

14 August 2025

> I sharpened my wit, my wardrobe, and my eye, and I made myself the most terrifying creature in any room I entered.
>
> *Lady Danbury, Bridgerton*

I can't help feeling a ripple of excitement thinking about how Adjoa Andoh and I will spend the next hour talking about kindness, acting, public life, private faith and reader ministry (and wondering if Adjoa will be anything like Lady D).

It is clear to me from the very start of our conversation that identity is important to Adjoa, as is politics and social justice. After quick introductions Adjoa focuses on current concerns and issues of social cohesion: 'We don't talk about poverty enough.' She continues:

> Britain doesn't quite know what it is any more. Brexit has sharpened that because we don't make things that give us a national identity, and we can't go out and colonize and conquer, which also gave us an identity. I don't think we can solve anything to do with the state of the internal cohesion of the nation until we address that fact. Confident people who are clear about who they are are much less hostile to people who are not their people being present. But when people haven't got a sense of identity they can feel as if what they do have is being diluted. I think it's perilous, people having nowhere else to go with their frustration – they have no confidence in politics or politicians or people listening to them.

And suddenly we are into it:

> Kindness is so countercultural because kindness doesn't go with twenty-first-century capitalism. Kindness isn't about winners and losers. Kindness is about developing a sense of mutuality. And a sense of empathy.

Adjoa insists that kindness is an action, it is an active movement towards social justice. 'Kindness is a muscular thing,' she says. 'It's not soft, it's not squishy.' She contends that Christians have a particular calling to live lives led by kindness – the way we shop, the way we consume, live day to day, relate to each other, make ethical choices in all aspects of our personal and communal life. Adjoa explains more about her kindness practice. Though she has now stepped down from being patron of Fairtrade Foundation[1] she is still committed to the ethos of their work:

> I'm now the patron of a charity called TreeAid.[2] It is about taking tree planting techniques into communities where climate change is adversely affecting people's livelihoods and where trees can be nature's own corrective. I've been to communities in northern Ghana and spent time with the farmers and seen the way they work. Local Tree Aid advocates are pouring kindness back into the planet, pouring kindness into people's lives, and transforming the economic chances of communities, particularly the women because they're the ones who tend to do a lot of the labour-intensive agricultural work.

This commitment to kindness is also present in her creative work. As an actor and director, she values kindness in the artistic process of the collective performance space:

> If I'm directing I understand that I will have a much better time with my cast and crew if everyone has *buy-in*. That means everyone has to feel like they have *skin in the game*, that their voice is heard, their opinions matter, it's a collective endeavour and that the goal we're working towards is one. I might have the initial vision for it, but any leader that doesn't pay attention to the people they're working with is an idiot. People function better when they feel happier, and when they feel seen and heard and are a meaningful part of a collective.

This sense of collective thriving is one that Adjoa also applies to her ministry as a Reader in the Church of England. Being welcomed and being seen is vital to her vision for a church community life. When George Floyd was murdered her church put up Black Lives Matter banners and recently it extended a deliberate invitation to LGBTQ people. While she recognizes that this may be hard for some Christians, the intention is to be inclusive rather than divisive. For Adjoa, this is a matter of inviting people to be part of God's kingdom: 'Proper active kindness is about making the space for each unique soul.'

Adjoa argues that 'God's kindness needs courage and conviction and a sense of risk'. She challenges me, 'What will you risk for kindness?'

There's a pause as I reflect – what *will* I risk for kindness? Then in comes another challenge: 'What will *the Church* risk for kindness?' This is a moment of reckoning. Adjoa lists the risky business of forgiveness, restoration, acceptance, leaving judgement to God, transformation, colonial power. 'Just being alive can be a brutal business.' And the Church, the people of God, communities need to speak kindness into this brutality and, in Adjoa's words, to 'take it back to human souls'. She asserts that the Church can only do this by 'getting our own house in order'.

> What do we do about our investments in horror, in slavery, in arms? What's a reparative story there? You can preach, you can proselytize, you can be God's hands and feet. But we have to acknowledge that we're cracked vessels. That's a fantastic way to welcome people in, to acknowledge our own dysfunctionality – only God is perfect. We're all in the weeds, struggling as we do, but if we can apply this lens of kindness to that struggle then we can begin to get somewhere authentic and truthful.

Adjoa concludes: 'We believe in a God of healing and transformation, and second chances, and seventy-seventh chances, and that is part of kindness. It's demanding work, but it's rewarding work – it's a rewarding way to live.'

Yes, it is a rewarding way to live. Brave, risky – but what an adventure!

4

Dignity

Winnie Varghese, The Cathedral of St John the Divine, NYC

20 August 2025

> The quality of mercy is not strained;
> It droppeth as the gentle rain from heaven
> Upon the place beneath. It is twice blest;
> It blesseth him that gives and him that takes
>
> *William Shakespeare*[1]

Winnie Varghese is on the cusp of a new ministry. She is about to be installed as the twelfth Dean of the Cathedral of St John the Divine, New York City, and has recently moved. When we meet Winnie is sitting in her home office in New York still surrounded by boxes.

I ask Winnie what kindness means to her. 'It isn't a primary value in the USA,' she says. Kindness implies a polite nicety yet the biblical Hebrew word *hesed* is usually translated as mercy and as such it has 'legal implications'. We discuss cultural differences: Winnie explains that in her experience 'niceness' appears to have cultural value in the UK. She continues to explain that this is not the case in her Indian culture, where to be 'kind' might be considered a rudeness as it is construed as a performative act. We move on to contemplate what kindness might mean in a more generative sense – how can kindness be understood as practice? Winnie suggests that kindness, as encapsulated by the word *hesed* or 'mercy', is about the propagating practice of dignity. It is, suggests Winnie, about living out the understanding that all of creation has dignity:

> I think a foundational piece of being a Christian theologically is dignity. Dignity ... it's a profound word. Dignity in ourselves is not something anyone gives to us. It's in the old ordination ... They say *Dignus Est*

> before they proceed in ordination – 'You've answered all your questions, which means you are worthy, that you have dignity.' It's a foundational Christian understanding that all of creation has dignity. No one can give you your dignity, they can take it from you. No one can really hand it to you. So, one of the ways I just literally claim that every day is to stand in dignity and to treat others with dignity.

The proliferation of dignity requires a sacrifice and a handing over of power as well as an assertion of rights. Winnie stresses that as a South Asian queer woman from Texas there is an expectation that she will perform in a particular way:

> We're supposed to be kind to everyone. We're supposed to be endlessly kind and giving and offering and self-offering, and we're supposed to care about mercy and justice and sacrifice for it. In many ways, I am absolutely acting out my gender.

But this is who she is and who she wants to be – this is Winnie. She has claimed her identity. She has a right to be this person, even in a role that might usually demand a different set of behaviours and a different visual identity:

> Our catalogue version of an Episcopal priest is a really tall white guy with grey hair; he's really elegant, probably very handsome; his clothes are a little bit older than they should be; he smiles at you, and he doesn't have to, he sees you, right? So, I'm very aware that that isn't what's happening when my body does that.

So, what is the kind response to identity expectations? Well, Winnie asserts that the only authentic response is to act with dignity and offer kind dignity – to be polite and reflexive. Winnie feels that she must insist on being grounded in order to be herself in role:

> I think kindness is very grounded, and heart and gut connected. So my colleagues are very much performing their roles – God bless them – because it's all they can do. You can feel the brittleness in that, and you can see it, and part of what happens is literally, I think, people put their heads down. They even put their heads down when they're looking at their laptops, and they don't answer their emails, and they're overwhelmed, because they're not grounded ... The pressure becomes

defining and that person is easily harmed. I think kindness is being more grounded in our spiritual practice, acting out of our humanity.

To persist in this way of offering kindness in dignity, to self and others, is a way of acting truth and justice. This is a grounded justice that creates space for inclusivity and extends love. Winnie asserts that it is not kind for anyone to be 'on their knees'; to allow ourselves to be subservient or defined by role, class, culture, race, gender or sexuality is an unkindness to self. To do this to others is an intolerable unkindness.

Winnie implores us: 'Live as faithfully as we can in the times that we're in.'

5

Protection

Martin Poole, priest and author

21 August 2025

> Some believe it is only great power that can hold evil in check. But that is not what I have found. I have found that it is the small everyday deeds of ordinary folks that keep darkness at bay. Small acts of kindness and love.
>
> *J. R. R. Tolkien*[1]

Martin Poole is a priest in the Church of England and serves in a parish in Brighton. He's an author[2] and founder of Beyond Church.[3] Martin and I worked together at Greenbelt for several years; he led the curation of worship at the festival, and I assisted. We share a love of creativity and alternative worship. As we catch up on Martin's current work and how he is seeing kindness emerge in the context of parish life, it becomes apparent that he is creating a kind environment by being the person who sets parameters and offers safety:

> Giving people clear boundaries is an important part of that kindness for me. An important part of my role recently has been stepping in to help people in distress. I'm protecting them as well as those around them. We have a particular client who comes to our lunch club who has serious mental health problems and is incredibly verbally abusive. I have become the person to step in and manage him, and so now I am the gatekeeper. So that everybody else feels safe in the space.

Being serious about risk and safeguarding is more than policies, it is about how practice is enacted in the present. For those at risk of harm this is a profound kindness – offering protection is significant to those who are unused to being taken seriously. Martin's care is particular, but not unusual among parish priests. There are churches across England that day in and day out offer safe places – Places of Welcome,[4] lunch clubs, knit and natter groups, pram clubs, etc. – and church halls that open their doors to other charities that work with the most vulnerable in our neighbourhoods. In Martin's case, the church he leads is used by many groups that require this level of attention and kindness. So, I ask, what does personal protection look like for Martin? How does he maintain kindness for himself?

> Through my own support networks, previous friends, who are outside of these situations. I would call them networks of support kindness. There's something about understanding my own resilience, my own emotional and spiritual resources and whether I'm capable of taking on those things. That's being kind to myself. Saying, 'Can I cope with this kind of situation?' And, if I find it's beyond what I can cope with, how will I get support? I know who I would go to.

The framing of kindness here is that of self-care and self-awareness. Martin is an experienced priest: he's been ordained for over 35 years and in this parish for 15 years – he knows his gifts, skills and talents, and he also knows his limitations. Kindness is a clarity of boundaries and appropriate levels of protection.

6

Letting go and letting God

Guy Hewitt, Church of England Director for Racial Justice

22 August 2025

> God is love, and all who live in love live in God, and God lives in them.
>
> *1 John 4.16* (NLT)

Guy Hewitt is the inaugural Director for Racial Justice in the Church of England. London-born of multiple heritages, he is an ordained priest living in Brixton. When we meet, the work of the Racial Justice Unit (RJU) is going through some changes and a new governance board is being established. He is facing a significant reduction in funding while also celebrating the significant gains in the anti-racism work that they have initiated, funded and instigated.

These are uncertain times for the work of social justice in general and as we begin our kindness conversation we are both feeling a little heavy-hearted. He shared:

> I am writing an article for The William Temple Foundation on the fortieth anniversary of *Faith in the City*, focused on social inclusion, specifically on racial justice.[1] The motivator for this has been considerable resistance within some circles of the Church of England for the work on racial justice and Project Spire;[2] there has been more vitriol directed towards this work than any other area of belonging and inclusion including Living in Love and Faith. The challenge is keeping the faith against tremendous opposition.

Social inclusion and the growing polarization in British society is a concern that Guy and I share. We began to talk about a project we are developing in Liverpool and elsewhere as a response to the riots that occurred after the devastating attack on a dance class in Southport where three children died and others were critically injured. When the attacker was arrested, his racial and ethnic identity were incendiary, feeding the flames of xenophobia, Islamophobia and anti-refugee and anti-migrant sentiments.

It felt like nobody was listening to each other: tension around immigration, asylum seekers, grooming gangs, the cost-of-living crisis, a growing acceptance of toxic masculinity, talk of incels, and negative blow-back around 'wokeness', created a perfect storm that led to street violence and rioting. We saw angry, mostly white, young men, burning a library in Liverpool, looting and attacking mosques, and goading police lines.

The places where rioting happened are largely 'forgotten' towns, unemployment is high, child-poverty is a serious concern, and the Home Office is increasingly using them as cheap housing stock to accommodate asylum seekers. At a time when the nation needed a church that was confident in its identity as a trusted voice in public space, where 'the cure of souls' means all souls, sadly the Church of England was largely mute. When a deeper level of the interrogation of inequity was required and open conversations about Britishness, social cohesion and the common good were urgently needed, we didn't speak up.

These are complex times and Guy and I recognize that we are feeling as though the work we do is not easily seen or understood for trying to make our country better, safer and more unified. We battle away in the background trying to raise awareness of the work for justice, which is often misinterpreted as political correctness, or lands as unpatriotic or being contrary, when what is being advanced is the love command, specially 'the love of neighbour'.

Guy reflects on our conversation in relation to the importance of kindness in all this:

> We must keep the faith because we believe that unity and inclusion are God's work which, according to Revelation 7.9, is where the Spirit is leading us as the Body of Christ. But it is easy to become despondent in this dark and difficult time ... but I shouldn't say dark, because it's not all that dark; yes it is a difficult time, but conversations like this and talks of kindness become a breath of fresh air that allow the Spirit to dispel the darkness, and to remind us of the challenge of this journey which is ultimately the way of the cross, and a challenging process of self-emptying as we learn to truly 'let go and let God'.

Then, injecting a bit of levity into our conversation, Guy recounts the tale of a Christian who in despair cried out to God: 'Lord, I can't do this any more.' And God answers: 'Finally! Now I can take over.' Guy goes on:

> Let us consider the Samaritan whom we call 'good'. I am sure he would have been challenged in terms of his own inclination to say, 'Oh, to hell with this. I'm not going and helping this Jew who would otherwise despise me. I'm not going to clean him up, see to his wounds, and pay for him to be looked after. If his own, the priest and Levite, could walk away, then why not me ...'
>
> There are many legitimate reasons why the good Samaritan could have said, 'No, this is not happening.' But what permeates through this narrative is his ultimate love of God and the outworking of agape love which compels him to say, 'You know, this is my duty – to God and my neighbour.'
>
> This is why the narrative focuses on the Samaritan, the scorned and marginalized, because our Lord Jesus Christ seeks to underscore that the good news imbues a radical counterculture of love. By starting with the priest and Levite, he focuses on those who can find legitimate, institutional reasons not to act; those who cross the road, who say, no, we shouldn't, we can't, we won't ... we have just cause not to get involved. Those who would seek to wash their hands of a situation without realizing that their faithlessness renders them more unclean in the eyes of God.
>
> I believe, as Martin Luther King Jr opined, the ultimate test of our faith and love occurs not where we stand in moments of comfort and convenience but at times of challenge and controversy.
>
> The Samaritan goes beyond the institutional and sociocultural limitations and obeys the love command ... the key to this, that golden key to kindness, is that kindness doesn't come from us but is generated through the love of God which compels us to proclaim a social gospel (Luke 4.18) of good news to the poor, release to the captives, sight to the blind and freedom to the oppressed.

Our conversation ends with a sense of solidarity. In our diversity, Guy and I have found a place of communion. We have shared some disappointments but once again we dare to dream of a hopeful future. Guy recognizes that the challenge is to keep focused on the source of kindness:

> It is about how able am I to let go of my challenges, my frustration, my uncertainties, and let God work through me, using me as his instrument of kindness, so that even when I don't feel worthy, like St Paul, the self-proclaimed chief of all sinners, I can find comfort in the fact that God has chosen me, with all my imperfections, to be an instrument of kindness to help a wounded world heal and to walk by faith, in hope and with love.

7

Recognize and resource

Ash Barker, URC Minister and Executive Director of Seedbeds

4 September 2025

> I find it helpful to think of kindness – charity – as a hard-headed discipline: a motivation rather than an emotion; frame of mind; a way of being in the world. It looks at human problems and seeks a way to fix it – not because the heart melted or the spirit groaned in the face of poverty or suffering or any sign of distress, but because this is the normal, natural way for humans to behave in response to the needs of others.
>
> *Hugh Mackay*[1]

Ash Barker is a United Reformed Church (URC) minister in Winson Green, Birmingham. He is also the founder and Executive Director of Seedbeds, an international Christian leadership organization.[2] Ash came to the UK from Australia in 2014 following 12 years of ministry in Bangkok. He and his wife Anji and their children have now made Birmingham their home and have an active ministry to their local neighbourhood.

Our meeting begins with a delightful frenetic energy that sets the tone for the whole kindness conversation. Ash can't find a stable internet connection, so, as we talk, he is wandering through the church, slowly making his way to the basement where the main router is. As he descends what seems like endless flights of stairs, he introduces me to team members and shows me around the vast space that is used by the local community. There is a busyness about the church that is both inviting and inspiring. So much of this appears to emanate from the energy Ash brings to the ministry. He tells me that his inspiration to serve came from Tony Campolo, who remained a mentor until his death in 2024. Ash owes much to Tony Campolo, who supported Seedbeds, Change

Makers and Red Letter Christians UK. As Ash tells me story after story of social action and missional work he's initiated or been involved in, I realize that his definition of kindness is of active engagement in the lives of people he meets in the communities in which he has lived. For instance, as he reflects on the kindness he and Anji experienced living in a slum in Bangkok, he relates the story of a woman named Poo whom they helped to start a cooking school,[3] a business that was to become very successful. He tells me:

> A lot of community development workers want to do needs analysis and find out what's wrong with people and what's wrong with the community. But discernment and kindness is about finding what's *right* with people, what's strong with people, where people's passions and gifts are, and then creating opportunities for that potential to be released.

These are the kindness principles on which Ash bases his practice. Ash appears to have developed a holistic approach to his entrepreneurial mission action. He might be a URC minister, but the Anglican Five Marks of Mission[4] are evident in his missional methodology. He places importance on the nurturing of faith and leadership as a profound act of kindness for the Church and the mission of God. This is as important as the social action that naturally emerges from the concerns of the neighbourhoods. He explains:

> I really wanted to be based in one place, and keep learning and growing as a practitioner, seeing how far this kind of asset, strength-based approach could go, but then be connected for local community leadership development. John Perkins[5] had this line: 'We really need relocators, people like yourself and Angi, who can relocate into communities and be intentional about change.' We also need remainers, people like Poo, who would stay, even though they don't need to. But we also need returners, and he was a returner. John grew up in Mississippi and his ministry took him back.

So the basis of his socially active community-based kindness is as a 'relocator'. From this church in Birmingham and Newbigin House where he lives with his family, Ash connects and enables real social change to emerge instinctively. Ash explains:

> If you live here and you're willing to be based here and dig in deep and you have that sense of hope and kindness as a centre, you can then be

> responsive, and you can then, you know, create momentum for change from within.

This take on kindness as community-led social action that is hyper-local is inspiring. Towards the end of our conversation Ash sums up our conversation: 'You can only share the kindness that you have, can't you? And it is kind of a channel of kindness, rather than a deposit of it.'

8

Imaginative breadth

Richard Coles, broadcaster, priest and author

8 September 2025

> When we choose to behave kindly, we shouldn't worry if our motivations are mixed. Advocates for kindness might do well to throw out the very concept of pure kindness – or even 'grading' levels of kindness according to some scale of selfishness – and instead argue that any extrinsically kind act 'counts' as kindness, irrespective of its motivation. For the longer our list of different motivations for acting in a kind way, the more likely we are to act – and that's what matters.
>
> *Claudia Hammond*[1]

Richard is not sure he is a kind person. In which case, I wonder, how he would define kindness. 'Well,' he replies, 'I think, not being an arsehole.' He continues:

> You try not to be an arsehole. One of the marks of arseholery is a significant failure of kindness. There are different forms of kindness – one version of kindness is the capacity to enter imaginatively into the reality of another person, and then do something. So, it's making an effort of imagination.
>
> Some people just have it, don't they? But I have to make an effort. Then once I have tried to imagine what it's like to be that other person, I try to think about something I might do to their benefit rather than detriment, if that's available to me. If I'm being an arsehole, I don't even see the reality of the other person, because I'm consumed with my own self-regard. But I think a lot of it is trying to dial down your self-regard and dial up your awareness of others.

To enter into the imagination of another person is quite a sophisticated framing of kindness and one that I am keen to know more about. How does Richard practise this kindness?

> Sometimes if you manage to put your self-regard to one side – if you can – that opens up frequencies in which God would broadcast to you in ways which would enlarge your understanding and your sympathy and your creativity. In such a way as to do something that might be of benefit to somebody else.

Richard goes on to suggest that kindness is more straightforward when you have privilege and relative wealth. He enjoys being generous and assisting his friends and family and various charities he supports. Wealth, he contends, helps to enable this kindness to be spontaneous and while it costs financially it rewards both the giver and the receiver practically and emotionally. This kindness creates a connection and an ongoing commitment to relationship and flourishing. But Richard is also aware of the potential of kindness to foster a false sense of pride, self-satisfaction or distraction:

> This is a really important thing here, isn't it? The kindness returns such a flattering reflection to ourselves that we have to be careful. One of the real big moments of revelation: I have a friend who is a very tough-minded person, one of my closest friends, I love him very much. One of the reasons I love him so much is that he is not scared to share his opinion, and he is a perceptive person. His father died ... he was devastated by this, and he phoned me up telling me that his father had died, and he began to cry, and I'd never ever heard this guy cry before. I was affected by it, and I said, 'Listen, J, come stay with us,' because he was on his own ... And then he paused and he said, 'Oh, you're really getting off on this, aren't you?' And I thought ... he knows me well enough to know that my instinct to kindness is, in a way, a means of mitigating arseholery.

As Richard tells this story I recognized that trait, I understand the tendency to 'do good' as a distraction – like a magician with a card trick. Perhaps if I do this kindness, people won't notice how broken and corrupt I am. But here's the thing. Both Richard and I (and I suspect you as well) know that no number of kindnesses will be enough to mitigate the reality. So, why bother? Perhaps because kindness is an overwhelming compulsion, a response to grace, to love, 'because love is never strictly metered'. Richard goes on:

> I think the more fully we live our lives to God, then the marks of God's reality will be evident in our lives, and one of those would be that endless capacity to live another's life. To make the judgements that we all have to make, but with a measure of generosity, and love and charity. One of the things I love about being a priest is that we have to be that with people who live beyond the horizon of everybody else's sympathetic engagement.

'Love is never strictly metered.' I couldn't stop returning to this thought. How many unmetered kindnesses have been offered? How many unknown exchanges of mercy? How many unmarked gifts of imaginative connection made?

Richard tells a good story ... so, I will end with one that excellently made his point:

> A guy I knew, who I was an ordinand with, he had had a terrible time. He had been one of those blokes who'd been abused by clergy in Wales, and when he had brought this to light, the church typically tried to close him down and made his ordination harder rather than helped him. Anyway, he sorted it out in the end, and he was accepted for training. Then he got this letter. It was just a three-line letter from Rowan Williams, saying: 'I just saw today that you'd been accepted for training, I just want to say how happy that makes me, and that I wish you every blessing as you do this.'
>
> What was really interesting about it was the date of the letter. It was the date of his enthronement as Archbishop of Canterbury. What presence of mind, what generosity! What imaginative breath, that on the day he was being consecrated Archbishop, he wrote that letter.

Love is never strictly metered.

9

Hopeful truth

Jayne Manfredi, deacon, author and broadcaster

9 September 2025

> The secret of salt and radiating light lies in their unadulterated truthfulness and clarity. God's city on the hill has a concern and responsibility for all aspects of life, and for people in the most distant places ... It serves the whole of life without letting itself be enslaved. It fights against all suffering and injustice without succumbing to the suffering and becoming unjust itself. It has to remain salt and light, for the seed of the future age lies hidden in it.
>
> *Arnold Eberhard*[1]

I am speaking to Jayne as she sits in her office space in the house she shares with her husband and four children in Crewe. Jayne and I had planned to meet in 'real life', but real life got in the way, and I wasn't well enough to meet her in person, so we flipped our plan to Zoom. I read Jayne's book, *Waking the Women: Faith, menopause and the meaning of midlife*,[2] and had an inkling our menopausal minds would click. Also, Paul Bayes (former Bishop of Liverpool) encouraged me to meet Jayne, and he was right – we got along famously from the moment we began to chat. Her informality and confidence struck me, as did her Madonna (the pop star Madonna, not the Mother of God) smile. I like her. She's honest and engaging, and kind. This is the point, isn't it – to speak to kind people and find out what makes them kind?

Jayne has fought hard to remain kind, to remain connected, faithful and present. She is an advocate for what she refers to as 'radical kindness', which she admits is difficult in this horribly punitive age; an age obsessed with social media, cancel culture and a political purity. These obsessions have infiltrated the Church. Christian public thought and culture are rife with a way of speaking that shuns and isolates those who do not share our theological sensitivities. This othering is not limited to a particular theological position. We all seem infected by it. Liberal, conservative, catholic – we all have allowed the worst of public discourse to drive us apart.

As Jayne reminds me, it's easy to be kind to the people that we feel we ought to be kind to. But how do we show kindness to the people who don't deserve it? As we continue to share our experiences of this division and the pain it has caused us, our families, our churches and even at times our own faith, it is evident that Jayne is determined to 'cultivate kindness' even when this feels impossible. She reminds me that it 'is not kind to lie' and that 'prioritizing process over people is wicked', and yet many of us feel we have experienced this in our professional and personal lives as Christians in community. As a result of the challenges she has faced within institutional structures, Jayne no longer serves within a Christian community nor currently attends church. Jayne is committed to being salt and light. She feels she is a *deacon* to those outside the Church. She has faith and remains hopeful; her absence has begun a healing: 'And now, coming out the other side,' she says, 'I still choose Jesus.'

> And I still choose to have some kind of hope for the Church, some kind of settled hope. I don't know what that looks like. But I know that it's like that post-communion prayer, that, even when we were far off, God calls us home. So, I know that … I have hope in that. God's called me out of atheism and found me from a state of not believing at all. So, God has power, and God is with me, so I know that whatever I'm going through at the moment, I might feel outside of Christian community, but I still have hope.

I ask Jayne if she feels that kindness has sprinkled the path of healing. She replies:

> Yeah, definitely, and I know that's not the path that a lot of people who've been hurt by the Church take. I don't blame me for being angry. I don't want to misrepresent Jesus like that. The anger is not of God, because I think that sometimes it can be, but you can't stay there. It's not a productive emotion. Whereas I think kindness is. Anger breeds more anger, and kindness breeds more kindness, doesn't it? And that sounds twee, but it's true.

> What I needed to flourish was to just draw a line under it and try and get on with my life. And I have, I really have. I feel I'm where God wants me to be. And I want to honour God, by ... by flourishing.

What does justice look like? Well, for Jayne it looks like living well, being good, honouring Jesus and being free from the trapping claws of anger. Justice looks like kindness.

10

Creating space

Mim Skinner, writer and social enterprise founder

9 September 2025

> Until we realise that we all contribute to the framework in which crimes are committed and all have an interest in the redemption, restoration and reintroduction into the community of those in the justice system, then we will continue not to make progress, and the people in prison will continue to be one of our country's dirty little secrets.
>
> *Mim Skinner*[1]

Mim Skinner[2] is a writer and founder of the social enterprise REfUSE[3] – a food waste cafe/project based in Chester-le-Street, Durham. The last time I saw Mim was when she came to Liverpool Cathedral to offer our LDCSA Prison's Week Lecture,[4] based on her excellent book *Jailbirds*[5] in which she writes about her experience of working as a teacher with women in prison. Since I last saw her in 2019, she has had two children and, though she has changed the direction of her social action work towards food waste, she remains committed to working alongside those on the margins. Mim remains a calm, well-centred person who gently feeds her faith through social action and the seeking of justice.

I ask Mim what kindness means to her. 'I think it looks like the ability to quieten the self-voice, and to think about what another person would feel like, or what would they think, or what would they need?', she replies.

> So, in that way, it's a lot like empathy … not thinking less of yourself but thinking of yourself less. The times when I see myself being the most kind is when I've also left space. The times I'm most pressed, I see

> myself being the least kind, because I haven't got this kind of space and time for other people, and thought for other people; and the times when I've been quite inward ... I've felt less kind.

Mim addresses my questions with great humility. Her outward gentleness disguises an inner steely determination – for herself and for justice. Mim has worked hard to create a social enterprise that has strong ethics and standards. At the heart of the work Mim is committed to is what she describes as a 'posture of kindness'. She tells this story of a woman she knows:

> What I find mind-blowing is when one of the women – who I taught in prison, and I see regularly now – every time I see her, she's thought of my kids, and she's bought them something, and she comes out of her way to see me, and to walk a neighbour's dog. She's come from a care background, and has been in and out of homelessness, and that is just some horrifying kindness. Because I look at the way that I interact with the world. I've never been so inward as now – when I've had young kids in the last three years. And never thought of myself more in the last three years, and how I feel, and what I need than I have before. I'm just totally astounded by people who I see engaging with the world in a way that they are not been given to, but they still pour out in a pretty miraculous way. So, kindness is like a posture with which you meet the world.

I get the feeling that Mim's kindness is inspired by the kindness she receives from those who she encounters in these challenging spaces that she has initiated, whether it was as a creative teacher in prisons or in this new community project. Mim has a self-deprecating humility that belies her extra-ordinary competence and socially minded kindness. She is not do-gooding; this is the hard graft of re-using not only food that would go to waste but also people, actual human people, who have been shattered and spat out by the world as left like rubbish on the side of the pavement. Mim and her colleagues are creating space for kindness, for themselves and for others. She is also creating space for kindness stories to emerge and be told:

> I'm big on how narratives shape what happens. I'm a big believer in [how if] you tell a story of 'we hate this place, our high street is shit, everyone's antisocial, loads of antisocial behaviour, etc.', then that is what you sort of speak over a place. But actually, REfUSE draws people

> in ... it is amazing what people give to that place, and people describe it as their family. People volunteer full-time there, and that is partly because they were drawn to a story about 'this is how we treat each other', and they thought, 'well, I want to treat someone like that'. So, in some ways the story makes itself ... I am interested in the stories we tell about a place. And this is a kind place.

Mim is realistic about the challenges she faces and how hard it is to be kind in a world where the default appears to be unkind. She tells me about a homeless woman who constantly grumbles about the slowness of the menu preparation. Mim also recalls a recent incident where she had to make a formal complaint to the police about the way a Police Constable had dropped off a vulnerable young person to the cafe and expected her to take responsibility for him without any supervision or referral. While this is an unusual incident, it demonstrates how hard it is maintaining safeguarding responsibilities while working in a challenging environment. The hard graft of making kindness possible is evident in all these stories, which is why making space for them is so important – because these are the stories of the people who often go unseen, whose stories only get told in a negative way. Rebalancing the narratives is a vital kindness that can be transformative. Mim ends our time reflecting on how the Church could be more confident in telling the good news stories of kindness:

> There's definitely an element of telling the stories together as a community, but there's also providing spaces where it's the done thing to be kind – but be kind with confidence. I think the Church needs to sit in a place of recognition of those things, but be confident in that as well. Confident that we are being something, and modelling something, that is attractive, and is exciting, and we can tell this story about our communities.

11

The name of God is mercy

Charlie Bączyk-Bell, priest, writer and forensic psychologist

9 September 2025

> I believe that this is a time for mercy. The Church is showing her maternal side, her motherly face, to a humanity that is wounded. She does not wait for the wounded to knock on her door, she looks for them on the street, she gathers them in, she embraces them, she takes care of them, she makes them feel loved. And so, as I said, and I am ever more convinced of it, this is a *kairos*, our era is a *kairos* of mercy, a time of opportunity.
>
> *Pope Francis*[1]

Charlie Bączyk-Bell and I first met in 2024 when I interviewed him in Liverpool at a launch of his book *Queer Redemption: How queerness changes everything we know about Christianity*.[2] The book is clever and generous, as described by Sandi Toksvig: 'A clarion call to kindness. A thoughtful and well-argued piece that should be read by those with faith or without.' As well as being a writer, Charlie is an academic, an associate vicar in the Church of England and a forensic psychiatrist.

It was late in the evening when we began our kindness conversation – Charlie got in from work at 8.30 p.m., had his tea and kindly jumped on the Zoom call to me at 9.30 p.m. He is currently travelling two and a half hours each way every day to Broadmoor high-security psychiatric hospital in Crowthorne. He explains: 'It's a great job, but it's only for six months, so I'm tolerating the travel at the moment, but I'm just exhausted when I get up, exhausted when I go to bed.'

There is a gentle informality about the way Charlie and I speak about faith and our experiences of kindness. Charlie might be more known for his contributions to the ferocious debates about the Church of England's

Living in Love and Faith[3] process and the faltering decisions to offer same-sex blessings, but these concerns are not the primary topic of our conversation today. Instead, we begin by talking about how he experiences the presence of kindness in even the most intimidating individuals during his time in forensic psychiatry. When it comes to kindness, Charlie argues:

> I think many of [the patients I've seen] have never experienced the valuing of childlikeness in play; they've experienced it even less than many others have, and so, in a sense, for some people, the very first experience of it is not just the experience of kindness, but also the experience of being able to manage what it feels like for someone else to be kind, and the containment and everything else that comes with that.
>
> I realize that my emotional and spiritual privilege means that I haven't had to consider how hard it might be for some people to manage the containment and expectations of kindness. I rather take it for granted that kindness comes and goes, that it creates feelings and expectations in me, that I can create space around these things without becoming overwhelmed. I can give and receive kindness in a way that creates pleasure and a sense of achievement without my emotional capacity being over-stretched.

But Charlie notes that kindness is not a gift offered by 'nice' well-adjusted people. Kindness is far more complex:

> I think some people can be very kind in certain circumstances and then would never be necessarily described as a kind person, but can be incredibly kind, or can be described as a kind person, but then can be incredibly unkind.

Charlie continues:

> We want to split people, we want them to be good or bad, there's no middle ground. Kindness almost sparks its way through that neat categorization of good and bad. I remember a patient I had a long time back who died of natural causes but had basically a flippin' horrible history. I mean, a terrible, terrible history. And when he died, everybody in the hospital, the one thing they were describing him with was 'kind'. And I was, like, if you were the editor of the *Daily Mail*, the very last thing that you would do is call this guy kind. He was horribly manipulative. But the character trait which shone through was that he was

> able to be incredibly kind. That's fascinating ... You think, so what is it that then keeps that going in somebody's life? And of course, that's the other thing, the level of trauma and everything else that sits through. Basically, I have many patients that have had something really horrible done to them. That's not the same as saying that everybody who's had something horrible done to them does something horrible. But the level of recognition of trauma-informed treatment is increasingly there. It seems like kindness somehow ... sneaks in.

These reflections reminded Charlie of the writing of Pope Francis of the mercy of God (an excerpt of which is quoted at the start of this reflection), and the call to be kind – mercifully kind – even when faced with deep unkindness. I pray for the sneaking in of kindness. Kindness sneaking into our church and into each of us as we seek to discern our future.

12

Faithful improvisation[1]

Malcolm Chamberlain, Bishop of Wakefield

11 September 2025

> We must act in the appropriate manner for *this* moment in the story; this will be in direct continuity with the previous acts (we are not free to jump suddenly to another narrative, a different play altogether), but such continuity also implies discontinuity, a moment where genuinely new things can and do happen. We must be ferociously loyal to what has gone before and cheerfully open about what must come next.
>
> *Tom Wright*[2]

Malcolm Chamberlain has been Bishop of Wakefield since June 2025. Malcolm served as a Church of England priest in the Diocese of Liverpool for 14 years in a variety of posts before becoming Archdeacon of Sheffield and Rotherham in 2014. Malcolm was part of a small group that led 'Dream'[3] in Liverpool, an alternative worship fresh expression of church that worshipped in bars, nightclubs and other venues across the diocese, eventually landing at the cathedral. Dream offered worship that played into the idea of faithful improvisation and experimented with liturgy and form. So, it was interesting that Malcolm began our conversation about kindness with reference to Tom Wright and his five-act/kingdom hermeneutic.[4]

> It probably sounds very predictable and trite to say it, but I mean it from the bottom of my heart: my model for life in all its fullness is Jesus, and what we see of Jesus in the Gospels, and what is attested to Jesus through the Epistles. I think Jesus was the epitome of kindness in the sense of laying down his life, ultimately, for those that were hurling insults, beating him, and ultimately executing him. They were the very

> people Jesus was laying down his life [for], as you and I are. That's absolute kindness. But sometimes Jesus wasn't nice – he really did push the envelope, and challenge people, and call things out.

Of all the kindness conversations I have had I think Malcolm was the most Christ-centred. Indeed, when we started talking about Jesus, we both became proudly evangelical and buzzed off sharing our excitement about the gospel. Which is how we segway into faithful improvisation – a holy play on living the gospel for our time. Asking the challenging questions about how kindness, justice and truth work play out when we wrestle with the difficult issues that we face in the world (and the Church). Malcolm argued that without the foundation of the four previous acts, the fifth becomes a shouting space, a contested environment where listening is scarce.

> Tom Wright's point is we are now inhabiting part of this story. We know what's gone before and we know our endpoint; we trust that with faith all things will come to the kingdom. The kingdom will come on earth as in heaven, and that's actually original creation restored, however you understand that. But we are now inhabiting that place where that is being brought about, and God, by God's infinite grace, chooses to give us agency in the bringing about of that kingdom – and that's the amazing and exciting thing about the Christian faith. We are caught up in the very activity of God in human salvation – and the fact that it's not static, that every second counts. We're learning all the time as well, and I've often said in sermons ... Christianity is not a syllabus to be mastered or an exam to be passed, it's a life to be lived. Jesus didn't say, 'I've come that you may have your doctrine absolutely correct on day one, as soon as you invite me to your heart.' He said, 'I have come that you may have life abundantly, so you may know what it means to live as a human being in abundance in relationship with your Creator.' And that's an ongoing learning, refining experience as we grapple with Scripture, and as we grapple with the world in which we live. Bring them into conversation with each other.

You can hear the excitement in the way Malcolm speaks about the gospel and Jesus, that he is absolutely certain that we are all vital to the world and each play a part in the outworking of the kingdom of God. Without exception the kindness of God is that all creation will be redeemed and restored.

[Referring to John16.12f.] What if Jesus had said, 'I have much more to tell you ...' and then proceeded to tell them everything the Church and the Christian tradition has learned in the last 2,000 years, let alone what's ahead of us that we don't know yet? It would have absolutely blown their minds. They couldn't bear it. And there may still be things that we can't bear now, insights and truth located in Jesus that we're still grappling our way towards. It might mean a rereading of Scripture, it might mean a re-understanding of Scripture to get there, and I think this is particularly relevant to some of the debates that are live in the Church at the moment: are we finding our way towards understandings that we just weren't able to get to in the past? Is the activity of the Spirit of God in the wider world, is the Spirit of God doing something in terms of revealing to us something that previously we couldn't have accepted? If we believe in this, that we're inhabiting the story, and that we are good news, and that the good news is being told, even in our conversation now, something is being transformed. Because a new revelation is being gifted us. Every time you sit down and have a conversation with somebody, if you're genuinely listening, we're learning new stuff, and God is somehow in the mix of all of that. And here we are, living kindness because I'm learning about the different nuances of kindness in this gentle dance of faithful improvisation. If we don't do that collectively, as the Church, as the people of God, then we are limiting ... ourselves!

13

Sacred action

Tim Goode, Canon, York Minster

16 September 2025

How very good and pleasant it is
  when kindred live together in unity!
It is like the precious oil on the head,
  running down upon the beard,
on the beard of Aaron,
  running down over the collar of his robes.
It is like the dew of Hermon,
  which falls on the mountains of Zion.
For there the LORD ordained his blessing,
  life for evermore.

Psalm 133 (NRSV)

Tim Goode is Canon for Congregational Discipleship and Nurture at York Minster. His book *Breaking, Not Broken: Ableism and the Church after Constantine*[1] was published in January 2026. Tim is a fierce advocate for equity and inclusion, and his work in the Church of England synod and Archbishops' Council is testament to his commitment to engaging the institutional aspects of the church politic in social justice. Tim has been a great source of encouragement and solidarity for me as I slowly come to terms with the change in my mobility following a stroke. It is this kindness that kicks off our conversation. Tim explains:

> Kind is being kin. And if you're being kin you are seeking to imagine, as best you can, and inhabit as best you can … and understand the story of the person that you are in kin with. In that given moment. That involves really doing some work. You know, my friendship with you means I'm utterly invested in your flourishing and to play any part I can to enable

> your flourishing. I have to understand you and engage and enter into your story. And listen and hear it ... which is sacred.

I am drawn to this idea that kindness is a sacred action – as something might emerge as a human attribute that, when exchanged, has transcendent qualities. Tim continues to develop this idea as he points out that we don't know the 'hinterland of everyone we talk to' and that rather like Moses taking off his sandals when he approaches the burning bush,[2] these exchanges of kindness 'become holy ground'. He values 'the sacredness of each and every person's story' and is concerned that 'the catastrophe of the present culture wars is that it's all about shouting and nothing about listening'.

Kindness pours oil on the catastrophes of the present culture like oil on the head of Aaron.[3] Kindness is a source of cultural and social healing and creates a connection that begins to bring our life stories together. Tim considers this as a flourishing and the deepening of community. In this context human kindness reflects the 'immeasurable love, generosity and hospitality of God'. Tim contends that the telling and listening to each other's stories is vital to the living of the gospel in our time, and a profound sign of our kindness, because this is a way we can commit to each other's flourishing:

> We live in a world where there's pain, where there's suffering, where there's loss, where it can be profoundly unfair. We can also, therefore, be graceful. We can be generous. We can go beyond. We can be utterly altruistic. We can absolutely invest in the flourishing of Earth. We can really love as God loves us. We have the absolute capacity to do that. So for God to supernaturally intervene into that dynamic would be actually to rob us of the very gift of life. The very gift of being able to love freely And costly. Love is the ultimate expression of vulnerability.

At the heart of Tim's framing of kindness is that Jesus' life, death, resurrection did not hide away from the pain of living a human life. Jesus bore the suffering that people bear. His death was a brutal torture that left him scarred and disfigured. That these scars were not airbrushed out at his transfiguration – and as such his story is not fixed in time. Jesus is a broken, triumphant sovereign who continues to participate in and know our story:

> The resurrected body is the ultimate expression of vulnerability. It's the greatest exercise of the imagination that there has ever, ever, ever

> been. I think it's utterly extraordinary ... and it's why I'm a Christian. Because it's totally graceful. The idealized norm is static. You try to relate to it, but it does not relate to you. It's not interested in you at all. It couldn't give a damn. The only thing it doesn't like is vulnerability ... it doesn't like to be threatened ... it's only after its own survival. Whereas the risen body is all about holding your story, holding my story. It's completely storied. It's not static. Coming beyond death, the ultimate human experience which we will all encounter, means that it holds your story, it holds my story, it holds absolutely everybody's story. It's the ultimate expression of being held, heard, known. It is profound good news. I think God looks at us as story, not static.

Being seen as unfolding story is a profound kindness extended by God into humanity in Christ. We are called to extend that kindness by experiencing, understanding and living alongside each other in a non-static storied way. We are also called to know God in Christ as a living story, a gospel being outworked in our time in the power of the Holy Spirit. We all have a story to tell; this is our good news. A gift of profound kindness.

14

Rest is resistance

Kate Coleman and Cham Kaur-Mann, co-founders and directors, Next Leadership

17 September 2025

We can rest, build, and usher in a new way.

Tricia Hersey[1]

Kate Coleman and Cham Kaur-Mann are the cofounders and directors of Next Leadership. They state: 'Our mission is to transform leadership by equipping leaders to serve well in today and tomorrow's world.'[2] I first met Kate and Cham over ten years ago when they led a residential course for women in leadership based on Kate's book *7 Deadly Sins of Women in Leadership: Overcome Self-Defeating Behaviour in Work and Ministry*.[3] I have had the privilege of their mentoring ever since. In 2024 they joined our senior leadership team in the Diocese of Liverpool to lead us as we explored unconscious bias behaviours and discussed our anti-racist policy. Kate and Cham facilitate with great wisdom and clarity and offer the kind of group and individual coaching that leads to deep learning.[4] So, an opportunity to listen to their take on kindness helped me to appreciate the way in which stepping back and resting in kindness was a form of resistance: resisting what Hersey identifies as the dominant narratives of grind culture, a collaboration between capitalism and white supremacy.[5]

Hersey contends that this decolonizing[6] work is an endeavour for all people to engage with; we will all benefit from the loving-kindness of this sort of rest. As a person who has been racialized as white, I am listening to this wisdom from a place of privilege, and as such I must be attentive to my bias. I must be attentive and look at this through a different lens. Kate explains:

> Kindness is resistance in the current climate ... it's to resist the dehumanization, it's to resist the dismissal, the infantilization of people. Kindness has got to be injected back into the structures, into churches. We have allowed the place to be overrun. Jesus told us that would happen. I know he was talking about a human being, but if the spirit goes out, wanders about a bit, and then comes back and the house is not swept clean, it brings seven even worse spirits, and you're in real trouble, and it kind of feels like that's where the Church is, with this ...

Kate and Cham are speaking here about 'the Church' in the widest sense; they are Baptist ministers, but they work across all denominations. They have a great deal of experience of working in contexts that are not liberating spaces for Black and Brown people. They speak of 'killing with kindness' racist behaviours and negative encounters. Cham tells me:

> I can't explain it. It's quite visceral. You just know when someone is just spitting venom at you without the spit, although I've had that as well. But it's like they're not recognizing your humanity; all that you represent is anathema to them. And my go-to, then, is honouring the humanity of the person in front of me. And then I go home and weep and wail. But in the moment I go out of my way to be gentle and generous with them. I think that's really powerful. The antidote is quite simple: love.

I am challenged by what Kate and Cham have presented here. I feel an overwhelming sense of injustice and anger that my friends have had to experience such inhumane behaviours. It feels like the opposite of justice. I am uncomfortable. Kate and Cham often challenge my middle-class white sensitivities.

> I think all the opposites of kindness, or all the opposites of the fruit of the Spirit, particularly kindness, is banditry, you know, and we've been hospitable to them, to the very offices. We've created environments that have facilitated and enabled them, and we've said, 'Oh, it's OK', because the other stuff is too hard. What sacrifice are we making as Christians?

It is hard. It is hard to challenge the unkindness. But I can appreciate that responding to cruelty with violence or hatred, understandable though that might be, could be interpreted as a perpetuation or acceleration of brutality.

> Choosing to respond in a particular way that is so wonderfully demonstrated by Jesus and the non-violent stuff, like Martin Luther King Jr. You know, there are certain responses that just aren't gonna get you to where you need to get to. And it's not that I haven't walloped people once or twice, not physically, but in response to that kind of behaviour. But by and large, it doesn't actually get you anywhere and, you know, I've held so much primary and secondary trauma in my body that I'm actually beginning to notice it now, from stuff that's happened. But one of the things I can do is just refuse to become the thing I hate. I refuse to become the one who dehumanizes another in order to justify my treatment.

'I refuse to become the one who dehumanizes another in order to justify my treatment. I refuse to become the thing I hate.'

I want to repeat this over and over.

'I refuse to become the one who dehumanizes another in order to justify my treatment. I refuse to become the thing I hate.'

This is at the heart of *killing with kindness* resistance. It is the still point of rest as resistance. Saying no to becoming *the one who dehumanizes another to justify my treatment*. Rejecting it with the gentle-firm force of rest. Rest knowing that your own identity is not compromised or conformed by the brutality of another. Cham insists:

> I refuse to become someone who cannot see the image of God, the *imago Dei*, in another human being, regardless of how different they are, regardless of how differently they think. I refuse to become the person who adds to another person's trauma.

15

Care for cruel and kind

John Bell, musician, writer and activist

19 September 2025

Will you come and follow me if I but call your name?
Will you go where you don't know and never be the same?
Will you let my love be shown? Will you let my Name be known?
Will you let my life be grown in you and you in me?
Will you leave your self behind if I but call your name?
Will you care for cruel and kind and never be the same?
Will you risk the hostile stare should your life attract
  or scare?
Will you let me answer prayer in you and you in me?

John Bell, 'The Summons'[1]

John Bell is a member of the Iona Community. He is a writer, musician, Church of Scotland minister and activist. A reflective tenderness pervades our conversation; John is grieving the recent death of the former Iona Community leader Kathy Galloway just a few weeks earlier, and we are both conscious of our mortality and the desire to live more gently. It is a gift to be able to speak about kindness with John, his gentle wisdom is a welcome balm. We begin by reflecting on youthful anger as a motivating force for social change and justice:

> My first, maybe, five or six years, when I was ordained, I was in youth work then, and I had a great disappointment with the Church. Youth work had no great priority, and you were kicking against the traces all the time, and I was really quite angry. I think I realized that expressing anger does not help when it's all self-referential ... and it really was. I just felt that the work that my colleagues and I were doing wasn't being supported. I turned up in this office with a part-time secretary and no

> budget. And, for four or five years, when I worked for the Church of Scotland directly, before I moved to the Iona Community, that was the kind of thing you were dealing with. I realized a couple of times I would say something which was barbed, and people would react aggressively. And it was only after a while I thought, 'This is no use', you know? What I'm doing is I'm foisting my own sense of injustice on other people, and they can't deal with it. And I think that I realized that there's a difference between an anger which is a highly personal thing, which might come from disappointment, or jealousy, or whatever else, which, you know, makes you a very nasty person. There's an anger which comes because there is an injustice that affects everybody, and therefore you can speak out of our sense of solidarity and compassion, rather than personal animosity. And I think that was a big change in my life.

This truth chimes with me; one of the things I have noticed in the last few years, since my husband died, has been the tendency to treat all injustice with a similar outrage. I will have to check myself to measure my responses and try to act with kindness and compassion when faced with inequity and other social challenges. As the Director of Social Justice, this is an everyday experience, and I have become increasingly angry and frustrated, and as a result I have felt the way I influence has become harsher. John tells me his antidote to this: 'Poke fun at yourself. It's maybe a way in which you can endear yourself to people who otherwise may be suspicious or awkward ... I think that's a kindness.'

I agree with him. This is one of my ways of dissipating anger and frustration as well as connecting with people. We laugh at ourselves and with each other and there is a joy in our recognition. He offers this encouragement: 'Justice is the political currency of love,' John insists.

John connects with people, he listens, he remembers, and he empathizes. This is a kindness. He notes, 'You just have to develop a sensitivity as a priest or as a minister.' His empathy for others is evident in the stories he tells of the kindness he has received and instigated.

I am interested in what has been the kindest thing John has ever done. There is a pause. A space. A moment of intense emotional self-reflection. Then he tells me:

> Probably, coming out [as gay]. I did it at Greenbelt ... maybe eight years ago? It didn't completely change things, but I was always aware of a kind of shadow. All my friends and people who I've worked with knew. But because I'd held some positions in the church and because, to some extent, the resource group that I work with in the Iona Community

> depended on being financially secure ... I never earned any personal money. Anything we got, whether it was copyright or broadcasting, all went into a fund that paid for four of us. So, I was aware that if it were revealed, when I was in charge of the liturgical committee of the Church, or the new hymn book for the Church of Scotland, or just working with another three people, if it was revealed that I was gay in a public platform then that might jeopardize things that were important for other people, and so I held back. And then it was the suicide of a wee girl in Manchester which made me think, well I'm old enough now. You know, it doesn't really bother me what people think of me. So, I think that was a kindness to myself, yeah.

This is when I realized the importance of kindness to self. For John it was the liberation of being set free from 'a kind of shadow that might threaten my well-being, or my friendship, or other people's livelihood'. This must have been more than simply a weight off his shoulders – this is freedom. This freedom is kindness.

John has so many stories about the ways he has been caught up in kindness – I would love to share them all. Perhaps one day I will. But the kindness story that stuck with me is this account of his coming out. This one-time public moment of liberation and loving-kindness to himself.

16

The practice of love

Jenny Sinclair, founder and director, Together for the Common Good

19 September 2025

Come Holy Spirit. We welcome you here in our midst.
Govern our hearts and minds, govern every aspect of our time together.
Be in every thought and word; in every intention and motive.
Lord, we thank you for those who have been an inspiration to us.
Thank you, for calling us through the Gospel to work together, and for each other.
We pray for others working for the Common Good and for those who resist it.
Bind us together across our traditions and move our heart's desire closer to the heart of your desire for us.
Lord, give us the grace do your will, and make our mission a joy.
In the love of Jesus Christ our Lord,
Amen.

Together for the Common Good Prayer[1]

Jenny Sinclair is the founder and director of Together for the Common Good (T4CG),[2] a charity that is 'dedicated to civic and spiritual renewal'; T4CG aims to help people 'discern ways to build common good in the places where they live and work'. In the last few years, Jenny returned to live in Liverpool, the city of her teens, where her father, David Sheppard, was bishop. Following what she refers to as a rebellious time in her life, she converted to Catholicism in her mid-twenties. Jenny is committed to working across the Christian traditions and has a desire to see spiritual renewal in our time. I began by asking Jenny what kindness means to her:

> It means the practice of love, self-sacrifice, tenderness, honesty, generosity. Crucially, these are virtues that are fostered by interdependence – which is where it connects with my work. What we're seeing in our culture is the consequence of a very bad idea – hyperliberalism – which, in shorthand, you can call individualism ... and that is based on the philosophy of the 'unencumbered self'. In other words, the belief that the human being is fundamentally an isolated and a rights-bearing individual who goes through life seeking their own interest. That's completely at odds with Christian anthropology, which regards us as relational beings made in the image of God.

Jenny contends that the false anthropology of what she calls hyperliberalism has left society, culture and politics in a state of moral and spiritual disconnection. She believes that it is at the heart of the Christian calling to challenge and transform this reality – what I would term 'unkindness' – by reconnecting, rejecting individualism and reorienting to our *kin-ship* in God:

> If we're Christians, then we first of all have to understand what our view of the human being actually is meant to be. There's so much mission drift across the churches – a lot of Christians have just lost, or don't even understand, what lies at the root of our identity in God: our identity is relational. That for me is fundamental. Because if we're to understand kindness as something to do with the connections between human beings – if it is about how we thrive, how we flourish in relationship, if it is related to Christian concepts like self-sacrifice – then it is the opposite of being focused on the self.

Jenny drew on her reading of Paul's first letter to the church in Corinth where the writer discusses the characteristics of love:

> Love is patient; love is kind; love is not envious or boastful or arrogant or rude. It does not insist on its own way; it is not irritable or resentful; it does not rejoice in wrongdoing, but rejoices in the truth. It bears all things, believes all things, hopes all things, endures all things. (1 Corinthians 13.4–7, NRSV)

Jenny insists the intertwined nature of love and kindness is significant and that they 'cannot be decoupled from truth'. Truth and truth-telling are vital to authentic human connection and community. The key words in Jenny's Common Good vocabulary are drawn from Catholic social thought.[3] As well as 'truth', the term 'solidarity' is key to her. She explains:

> In this hyperliberal system, capital is unconstrained and can flow wherever it likes. This is liberalism's economic form. In its social form, I can self-actualize as anything I want – free of mutual obligations, I don't need you ... I don't need to consult you, it's none of your business. This has negative economic, social and spiritual consequences, because it's based on an anthropology which is flawed, where human beings are not seen as transcendent relational beings but items on a spreadsheet. It's a real mess, and that's why we see the unravelling in all the countries that have adopted this system. There are all kinds of psychological pathologies that come out of it too. That's why we see exponential increases in loneliness, especially among the young. They are sadly also more likely to distrust their neighbours,[4] less likely to borrow or exchange favours with people in their street. Our systems have evolved from this flawed vision of the human being. This is why we see a breakdown of solidarity.

Reciprocity is also key to understanding Jenny's understanding of kindness where, she explains, mutuality is at the heart of social connection:

> I think there's something really profound in reciprocity – in human connection – this is really important when we're talking about staying human. We can practise this in our everyday lives – intentionally making eye contact at the checkout, talking to each other at the bus stop, not looking at our phone all the time. And in fact, it can be a blessing when you're vulnerable – when you're physically vulnerable and you need help, because you're forced into the position of making human connection.

The importance of 'human dignity' and 'staying human' is another key component in the common good language. A challenge amid our lack of real 'connection' and 'solidarity' is that we can become fearful or repulsed by views that are contrary to our own and as such unable to discuss difficult concerns. Jenny explains:

> I think people are living in what we used to call echo chambers, so much so that they are consuming completely different sources of information. They've become accustomed to their own views being mirrored back to them. And so, when they encounter something really different, they have what Jonathan Haidt describes as the 'disgust response'.[5]

These disconnecting social, cultural, economic and political factors have a profound effect on our ability to understand ourselves as spiritually interdependent human people made by a loving God of kindness and truth who seeks our well-being in community. To be a Christian who reaches out and into the common good is to be countercultural. This, then, is a demanding and deliberate course of action that requires us to be wide awake to the signs of the times. Basically, Jenny explains, 'We need each other ... we need to listen to each other, spend time together ... you will not come up with workable solutions if you only work it out with people who agree with you.'

I have learned a great deal from Jenny over the years we have worked together. Her ongoing work with Together Liverpool[6] and her Liverpool Cathedral Micah Lecture[7] in 2025 have inspired me to dig deeper into my common good practice and thinking. This kindness conversation was no exception.

> So, to go back to the definition of the word kindness, I could say that the common good, or the practice of the common good, is the antidote to individualism, which is closely related to what you mean by kindness. So perhaps we're essentially saying the same thing, using different language.

Jenny argues that to be truly kind we need to meet with and enter into deep discourse with others, particularly those who think and speak about the world differently to us. We need to acknowledge and then burst our filter bubble in order to seek the common good. She suggests that Matthew 5.47 would be a suitable quote from Scripture to end our kindness conversation: 'And if you greet only your brothers and sisters, what more are you doing than others? Do not even the Gentiles do the same?'

17

Bedrock of kindness

Liz Edman, Episcopal priest, queer theologian and political strategist

19 September 2025

> In big and small ways, the shortest path toward social progress is built on nonviolence, empathy and inclusion. It is wide and welcoming, peaceful and loving. It seeks to see others, no matter where they stand on an issue, as fellow human being first.
>
> *Dorcus Cheng-Tozun*[1]

Liz Edman lives in New York, she is an Episcopal priest, activist and political strategist. Liz is the author of *Queer Virtue* (both the website[2] and the book[3]). In her own words, Liz has been 'igniting people's understanding of Christianity and queer life for more than 25 years'. Liz has been inspiring and encouraging me in my faith for ten years, and I love hearing her talk about the gospel and the gift of queer diversity. As Liz and I begin our conversation she immediately recognizes that I am struggling, burning out, and I need rest, the kind of deep rest that can only happen in the arms of God in a quiet place. It is this gift of insight and clarity that demonstrated Liz's natural kindness. Hers is the direct plain-speaking kindness of an activist and political strategist.

Liz wants me to be well, to attend to my well-being – physically and spiritually – and she realizes that this is not easy for me. She pleads with me to take time to rest and recoup:

> We don't know how long we're gonna have to fight [for social justice]. We don't know if it's months, or years, or decades. Ellen, take that time until February [for sabbatical]. Because we don't just need you today and yesterday and Wednesday and tomorrow … we don't know how

> long we have. We need Ellen Loudon to be healthy and strong and … we need you.

She hears my anxiety and grief, and she gently tells me how she's been building her strength:

> I've been doing, for a couple of years now, a course of somatic therapy, which is a discipline that has emerged out of trauma studies. And kind of like, *The Body Keeps the Score*[4] … the whole idea is that your body holds all the memories, all the traumas, but also just a ton of wisdom and joy. Somatic therapy is all about listening to your body speak. It is the best work I have ever done. I have been able to learn how to navigate situations that have vexed me my entire life.

Liz is enacting a kindness that demonstrates her theory that 'kindness is a specific moment' not a general thing. A person responds in a kind way to a situation or a person and this requires a constant repetition of intention. She speaks of the collect she prays each day: 'May I be a witness to your love.' This is an intentional invocation of a life pattern that requires focus. 'Kindness shows to the world this graciousness and care, the grace, just the sheer grace of here we are in another day. And somehow offer that to others.' Liz describes the varieties of kindness she enacts:

> I think there are different kinds of kindness. There is kindness that is directed at stepping in when somebody's struggling and showing a kindness. There's also random acts – like sharing delight and surprise with people. I really love that … even on the street, just handing people good energy. That's not transactional, there's absolutely no larger goal there. One of the things that's lovely about it for me is you always get good energy back … it's kind of like being what I imagine being a florist is like!

I tell Liz that yesterday I cried on my therapist because I just wanted someone to give me some flowers – for no reason, just because they loved me. My tears were an outpouring of grief (another one!) because I miss my husband. Then, when I got back home from my therapy session, I kid you not, there was a bunch of flowers on my doorstep. No note. Just a lovely bunch of flowers. I stood on the step and laughed at the absurdity of it. Then cried again. I told Liz that my husband was crap at sending me flowers when he was alive so for that and for obvious reasons I was pretty sure they weren't from him now he's dead!

The layers of kindness in this interaction are profound: me hearing Liz's mention of the joy of floristry; the openness of a relationship that allowed me to speak of my therapy and my grief; the kindness of the flowers; the kindness of laughter and the absurdity of my 'joke' about dead Mark sending flowers. Kindness is about laughing with a friend about the things that hurt, even if that friend is thousands of miles away!

Liz describes this as a 'different language, a different kind of community'. She says:

> What is being demanded right now of us is a different kind of community building. What's being demanded of us is the creation of spaces where people's struggles really are truly recognized and we can somehow come together, not in an ideological sense, but as human beings, somehow come together in community to find a different way, a better way of living together. Undergirded by a commitment to treating each other with decency and respect and, yes, kindness.

I long for this type of community. To see that in our differences, and to feel the struggle of life together. I sometimes feel like some dolly-daydreamer who is idealistic and foolish. But surely this is the hope of the gospel, the call of the coming kingdom – to dream and act on these fantastic ideas about the common good, love and kindness. Liz speaks of kindness as a gift with a 'mysterious nature'. Like a treasure in a field that we discover and then go out and buy the whole field.[5] It is an 'interpersonal building block' on which relationships are fostered. 'Kindness becomes a bedrock. It's something you can look back on ... one thing to hang on to hope.'

18

(Kindness is) the gentle weapon

Andy Flannagan, singer-songwriter

22 September 2025

> Kindness. Yes. Be kind. Accept one another. Stand up for others. Celebrate those who might be different, seem different. Not just celebrate them: listen to them, learn from them. Fight for causes that you believe in. Your planet, your country, your community. They all need us as activists you know. And it's okay to be angry at injustice but perhaps start with an act of kindness. That's sometimes even more challenging.
>
> *Bono talking to year six as they leave school, 2020*[1]

Andy Flannagan describes himself as an Irish ex-doctor and rabble-rousing singer-songwriter. I am meeting Andy the day after he's had a minor operation, so we are off camera and chatting informally about our various recent medical dramas. I begin by asking Andy what kindness means to him:

> I think what it comes down to is that in our fast-paced, functional, utilitarian world where generally what is successful, and what is profiled, and what is honoured is what works – what gets the job done. I feel the need all the more often to shout loudly from the rooftops that God cares ... The kingdom is an internal thing as well as an external thing. If you break down what we mean when we talk about the kingdom of God and that being the territory in which his rule and reign is fully surrendered to. The beautiful thing about that kingdom is that it's never taken by force ... The kingdom can only extend by a surrender.

This is fighting talk – but fighting talk with a peaceful intention. Andy recognizes that the path to glory is that of the emptying of self. He equates this outpouring to the giving into God internally and extending out with God's gifts externally. This is a very different sense of surrender than the idea of capitulation or submission – this is not a white flag of self-defeat. This is a taking up of a new flag for a gentle sovereign of glory and raising it in a land of love, graciousness and kindness. I like this territory.

Andy and I are talking in the weeks after flags started appearing on lamp posts. Territory marked and land divided. As an Irishman, Andy is well versed in the trauma of living in a land where nationality and sovereignty are contested. I have some experience of this as well: when I was serving in a parish in Everton, as 12 July got closer the streets were bedecked with flags (including the Red Hand of Ulster[2]). During that week the pipes and drums would play, and the Orange Lodge would march along the Catholic boundaries. A small enclave of Ulster in the heart of the mainland. It would make my Belfast-born, Corrymeela raised[3] husband shudder. Mark and I would stand with our Catholic neighbours at St Francis Xavier Church (SFX)[4] as the march passed by. Apparently, in days gone by the passing Orange Lodge marchers would throw stones at SFX. These days it's mostly peaceful, though the sectarian flags and pavement painting persist. After they march, the Orange Lodge members take the train to Southport and drink the day away by the sea, returning bedraggled and worse for wear on the last train to Liverpool Central station.

I do not relish the idea of English streets becoming contested spaces. I do not want to assert my nationality or prove my status. I do not like the thought of England or Christianity being weaponized against anyone – let alone a stranger. This is not the territory I want to defend. 'For the kingdom of God is not food and drink but righteousness and peace and joy in the Holy Spirit.'[5] I am fearful about how these issues of national identity and social cohesion are going to play out in our political systems in the future – issues that have been raised by others in this book, notably Guy Hewitt.

I ask Andy how he thinks kindness can influence the debates that are dividing us. He is keen to discuss kindness in relation to seeking the common good – a theme taken up by many of those I spoke to, most notably Jenny Sinclair. Andy spends a great deal of time working with parliamentarians and those who support mechanisms of local and national governance. To an outsider such as myself political systems appear to be combative and confrontational, so I am interested in Andy's views concerning how kindness and compassion operate in such environments and if there are examples of arrangements that work more effectively:

> In the National Assemblies, and in regional assemblies such as the Scottish Parliament, it is much less adversarial, because it's in the round. You look at the European Parliament, which is much less adversarial, because it's in the round. And, you've got the proportional representation happening there as well, or different variants of a voting system that produce less of an adversarial environment in the way that First Past the Post does. So I think we have good questions as a country to ask about our system, and the legacy of that ... It obviously puts a lot of people off from getting involved in politics, because they think, well, I don't want to be involved in something where I'd have to check in my faith at the door, or I'd check my brain in at the door, when they look at the kind of nonsense of Prime Minister's questions, for example. But the thing that has to be said loudly is that that only represents a small percentage of the week in Parliament. What you're not going to read about is all the cooperation in the committee rooms, all the chatting together in the bars and in the cafes, all the playing sport together that happens – the actual human interaction that does happen in that place.

Andy is making a key point here about how we enact kindness in informal environments, and it is in these spaces that change can happen. Yes, the decisions are made in the Houses of Parliament, but the legislation is drawn and relationships forged in the easy spaces of leisure and conviviality. 'Kindness is complicated', it 'cannot be coercive' or forced. Perhaps the role of the Church (and all people of faith seeking the common good) is to 'stand in the gap' and instigate or participate in dialogue that is taking place in these informal convivial spaces. That might mean opening doors to those who want to fly flags as well as to those who seek asylum.

19

The wideness of God's mercy

Fergus Butler-Gallie, priest, writer and social commentator

25 September 2025

> There's a wideness in God's mercy
> Like the wideness of the sea:
> There's a kindness in His justice
> Which is more than liberty.
>
> *Fredrick William Faber*[1]

Fergus Butler-Gallie is a Church of England priest serving in a parish in West Oxfordshire. He is a writer and social commentator. His latest book, *Twelve Churches: An unlikely history of the buildings that made Christianity*[2] was published in 2025.

Fergus insists that he doesn't think of himself as a kind person, and if he is kind then his is a 'practical kindness', by which I assume he means it is a *doing* not a feeling. My experience of Fergus is that, as well as being good with words and languages, he is also keen to be of use pastorally and responds when it comes to practical concerns. His work among the Roma community in Liverpool was impressive and compassionate – and his Czech language skills were invaluable. Perhaps this is what he means by *practical kindness*? He explains:

> The kindness I find most meaningful, and I find myself drawn towards, and when I have often, in very small ways, perhaps managed it, has been that kind of incarnate almost practical kindness that often comes with risk as well, that mirrors Christ. I suppose I am compelled by what Christ has done for me to love others even when that's difficult. It's the nature of me as a person; I've always preferred practical expressions of that.

> When I was doing work with the homeless in Liverpool, for example, I felt one of the reasons I used to walk around in my collar is that I am then compelled to be kind because I am reminded constantly by them. Christ tells me I should see him in them. That's a constant refrain. That I should see God in them. I'm walking around, that's the nagging truth that gnaws at my conscience and then compels me to kindness. I suppose it's something that I think is best done in practical, incarnate terms – best done with actions, rather than words, if I'm honest.

This compulsion to incarnational, practical kindness is of interest to me as it suggests an urge beyond the immediate control of the instigator. Kindness emerges from the depths of Fergus's core and emerges as an application or a response to social concerns of an individual or community. Grace, Fergus explains, 'is the ultimate act of kindness, I suppose, in that it reaches out to me even when I am in the midst of an unkind world and as an unkind person. And therefore, I'm compelled to do the best I can to reflect it. It's mirroring the incarnation of God.'

We discuss the need to retain 'dignity' in our receiving and giving of kindness. Fergus comments:

> If I have shown acts of kindness I've always wanted them to be on terms of absolute equal dignity. I don't want to delegitimize or dehumanize the person who's on the receiving end of it. It's a bit like at the end of confession when the person who has heard the confession says, 'And pray for me, for I am also a sinner.'

As Fergus describes the nature of the exchange of kindness it feels as though he's describing it sacramentally: a holy and humble action of self-disclosure and reverence offered or received in the presence of God. 'We are all the man who's fallen among robbers. We're all in need of that healing kindness,' Fergus muses. I wonder if there is an equality about kindness when exchanged in a way that is infused with the presence of Christ. Certainly, it 'mirrors grace' and can 'warm hearts' and 'restore'.

> When I have been on the receiving end of kindness, the kind of thing people have given to me, particularly at low, low ebbs have been just those little acts that do restore dignity. And, therefore, I think there's something profoundly holy in that because what that person is doing is restoring you to the status that you've always been in the eyes of God. You've always been known and loved and filled with dignity, but we live in a world where sometimes by the unfairness and injustice of

> it, or even by our own actions, we can diminish that dignity. And the people who have been kindest to me have always been those who have managed to restore that ... to remind me that I am known and loved.

Fergus reminds me of the hymn quoted at the start of this chapter – 'There's a wideness in God's mercy like the wideness of the sea.' God's mercy is everlasting.

20

Ambushed by kindness

Testament, playwright, beatboxer and rapper

24 September 2025

There are whispers, conversations in secret places,
And plans set into motion, and we are ambushed by kindness
Holding hands over city skies
Standing sentinel over sanctuary sleep
And even though we have buried Beacons beneath bad dreams
Compassion watches at the window
It is angels that crouch in shadows
Healing that waits for us
A conspiracy of LOVE.
Working just out of sight
Each of us wanting each of us to be okay.
It's not *THEM* it's *US*.
I'm alive. And that's a start.
And music. Music is ...

Testament[1]

Testament[2] is at home in West Yorkshire. I'm invited virtually into his kitchen-diner, and we skirt around the niceties of kindness as he cooks tea for his family. Occasionally he disappears into another room and talks from in there, reappearing with an onion and a massive pack of chicken pieces. At one point he squeezes a packet of sauce into the slow cooker and grabs a knife and spoon and says, 'Might chop an onion while I talk to you now.' I nod and agree that chopping an onion is completely acceptable. He's multitasking like a pro!

Testament describes himself as a 'rapper with an English degree', a musician, a world record-holding human beatboxer (and, charmingly, that's what's on his email signature). He has been writer in residence for the Royal Exchange, Manchester, and written plays for the Leeds Playhouse, as well as writing for Royal Court and Netflix. Most recently he's been surprised to be asked to speak and perform in Christian contexts such as Greenbelt and Liverpool Cathedral for Black History Month in 2025. When I ask about his style, he timidly remarks: 'There's often a spiritual element to the work, whether that is magic realism, or nods to something bigger than ourselves, God ...'

Testament is polite, generous and speaks freely about his upbringing in the Church of England, his coming to faith within an evangelical charismatic tradition and his slow but positive deconstruction into a more sustainable faith. He has valued being able to talk more directly about his faith again and perform outside the art and culture circle, though admits it hasn't been easy because, as he puts it, the 'church has got so much blood on its hands ... and a bad reputation, there is a casualty list of people who've been hurt by church, including, partly myself'.

I'm touched by his honesty; he smiles a lot as we share stories of our Leeds lives and the fast train to London. We make small talk, and I try to make big talk. But the talk of kindness gets smaller, somehow less dense, more like a meme.

I rally my thoughts and go in again from another angle, trying to find some depth. I rehearse my script saying: 'I think kindness isn't about being nice but about a radical commitment to justice and the well-being of the other.' At that point he looks straight at the camera – zoom, he's looking right at me – and says:

> It's funny, because of how I've been brought up, I associate kindness with whiteness. How perverse is that? All of a sudden, I feel like Colonel Brandon or Mr Darcy in a Jane Austen novel. Like, oh, he was such a kind man, because he had an income of £300 a year. And he got Marianne out of the rain and took her to a doctor, or whatever it is. Yeah, yeah.

There's a pause.

> I don't think you hear the word kindness in Black spaces that much. But it's also a very middle-class word. Middle class, it feels old-fashioned, feels very primary school-y.

This pulls both of us up.

Our 'nice' conversation changes.

It doesn't stop being *kind*, but it isn't nice any more.

It's something else.

It becomes robust.

He wants me to find another word. He doesn't like the word 'kindness' to describe the things I am talking about. But that word is important to me. After all, that is what my book is about. So, I try again to use the word – I *insist* on the word – 'kindness' to describe something robust and seeking of resolution, change, righteousness. I just keep on saying words. None of the words work. None of my synonyms for kindness make the cut.

I am repeatedly stumbling.

I feel like one of those plump, plain white girls in a Jane Austen novel.

It is time for me to stop and let Testament get his son from school and finish off the tea.

Testament makes me think about being white.

I sit with the word 'kindness' and write this reflection. I must write something quickly because I don't want to let time justify anything.

Has kindness been racialized white?

Has kindness been feminized?

Has grace-filled loving-kindness been conformed so effectively that it's passed the line of niceness into something far more malevolent?

21

The hostess with the mostest[1]

Kate Bottley, priest and presenter, BBC Radio 2 and Songs of Praise

25 September 2025

> A culture of kindness is one that allows individuals to practice self-compassion first so they can be equipped and strong to connect that to others, and it's one that is anchored in purpose. If we can come together in compassion and kindness, that to me is everything. It allows them to be vulnerable, to laugh and cry and be human.
>
> *Dani Savekar*[2]

Kate has one of the biggest smiles I have ever seen. The last time I saw her smile in person was for a Children's Society Christingle service at Liverpool Cathedral. Kate was game enough to dress up in the inflatable Christingle, I was not! I remember her kindness that day – the way she made those children feel welcome, the generosity she offered the staff and the time she gave to the Children's Society. So, when I ask Kate about what kindness means to her, I am not surprised when she responds that it's about being 'noticed, being seen'; kindness is 'remembering details' about a person's life and speaking to them in a familiar way. Kate relates to kindness as a connection, with an awareness that kindness is drawing people into a convivial space. This is clearly something Kate enjoys experiencing as well as offering. Being included and involving others is important to Kate and she enjoys creating welcoming spaces. Kate loves a party – I missed her fiftieth birthday party, but by all accounts it was a blast! I want to know more about what Kate feels when she experiences kindness. She explains:

> I feel it's a whole-body reaction, so it feels like being held. It feels nurturing. It's got echoes of motherhood in there, it's got echoes of being fed. It feels like ... like communion.

What a beautiful treasure this kindness is. How wonderful to know that this gift can make someone feel so comforted and whole. And what a privilege to be able to give this to others. We must ask ourselves why we don't long for this in a way that makes us insist on this kindness in all we do? Why isn't kindness a priority of priorities? Kindness has a unique potency. As Kate says, there is a 'strength in kindness', and it is like a party where the priest is the host:

> I really enjoy it. I'm making sure everyone's got their coat on, and everyone's got somewhere to sit, and the person who's coughing over there gets a glass of water, and that's what I'll do to host the space. Partly because my priestly vocation is about hosting space for people. It's about holding all that stuff and making sure everyone's fed with the Eucharist, and making sure everyone's baptized, and making sure they are part of this. And I'm hosting it. Someone once said to me, it's not our party, its Jesus' party, we're just handing out the canapés. That's really the core of my vocation, I'm there to take people's coats, hand out the canapés, make sure people have got a taxi home. It isn't my party, it's Jesus' party, but he's asked me to look after the guests.

Kate makes the point that kindness is an 'equal opportunities employer'. It is an equalizer that 'is powerful when it is perceived as being offered to someone undeserving'. She then recounts a newspaper article about women in protests:

> What I'm thinking about is that brilliant picture of the young Asian woman facing down racists, and she's just smiling and she's defiant in that smile, but she's not hitting back, she's not meeting anger with anger, she's just holding the space.[3] It feels like that picture ... That when somebody is raging against you, if you meet them with kindness and humanize them first, then that has an inherent justice in it. Because what the hope is, is that it will cause them to meet it with a kindness. I'll at least make them ask questions.

Kate is a great host and a person who can challenge injustice with her defiant smile. I love that she is in the public eye and can speak and act kindness into these places. I know she thinks she 'can be a ratbag' (her words!) but her kindness is a gift and her hosting a joy.

22

Just good enough

Liz Hassall, Archdeacon of York

25 September 2025

> The kinder and the more thoughtful a person is, the more kindness he can find in other people. Kindness enriches our life; with kindness mysterious things become clear, difficult things become easy, and dull things become cheerful.
>
> *Tolstoy*[1]

Liz and I shared an office when we were at theological college – an unlikely collaboration that was successful and joyful. She is one of the most patient people I know. Liz has clear boundaries, and her family life is important, so I am interested in how she keeps this balance and remains kind – to herself, the family and her role. She explains that what gets in the way of kindness is when she is 'too tired, or too busy and overwhelmed, or trying to do three things at the same time'. So, she tries to head those things off before they become too deep. Liz has also learned to accept that sometimes things need to be 'just good enough'.[2] She explains:

> One of my parishioners said to me, 'You work harder than anybody else we've ever had in these parishes.' Until then I felt that I was a bit of a flake. That really opened my eyes: 'Oh, other people are doing a lot less.' So, I think I slowed down a bit at that point because all I could see was the work there was to do, and just one person not being able to do it, so just trying, trying to do as much as possible, and that wasn't sustainable. And it took somebody saying there's another way to do it, and we don't expect this of you.
>
> It wasn't an easy thing to do, just allowing … a higher degree of imperfection … in myself. I think it ties in with some of the stuff about parenting. That trying to be a perfect parent and do absolutely

> everything right will not result in well-adjusted children. You need to be imperfect to allow them to be imperfect as well. And to be well adjusted. So, you know – you need to be just good enough.

I can see that this way of being kind – to self and others – allows for personal growth and space to wrestle with challenges without too much judgement. But I wonder how this works in community or within systems that demand perfection or at least legal regulation? Can systems be kind? Liz suggests that systems and structures are built around more formal agreements, and they are less likely to be kind, though they may be just and fair – which is a different sort of kindness. The legal aspects of Liz's role are demanding, so creating space and working hard at communicating difficult news and information to others in a clear and thoughtful manner is important. In many of these decisions she is 'balancing the kindness of the individual and the kindness to the community'.

> I come to that from the point of view of both justice and mercy being fundamental attributes of God. Seeing them played out in the life of Jesus. So, they are things that we should be concerned with. But I think ... I would say, as human beings if in doubt ... err on the side of kindness. Let God deal with the justice.

In the Gospels we often see Jesus choosing to offer kindness as a priority ahead of the law or everyday community justice. Examples such as Jesus healing on the Sabbath[3] and the woman caught in adultery[4] show us that Jesus put kindness ahead of legal obligations or social norms. Being able to discern the right and considerate way for us to act like this is not easy – we are not Jesus; we do not always have the moral or ethical authority to make decisions in this manner. However, I wonder if we still need to at least consider kindness as an option and build it into our systems and structures as a possibility.

23

A posture of kindness

Rob Wickham, Anglican bishop and CEO, Church Urban Fund

25 September 2025

> Jesus didn't say, 'Blessed are those who care for the poor.' He said, 'Blessed are we where we are poor, where we are broken.' It is there that God loves us deeply and pulls us into deeper communion with himself.
>
> *Henri Nouwen*[1]

Rob Wickham is a Church of England bishop; he is CEO of the Church Urban Fund (CUF)[2] and Chair of Housing Justice.[3] I am chair of trustees of Together Liverpool,[4] CUF is a partner of this charity along with the Liverpool Diocese, so we share many core principles in the way we seek social justice and engage in social action in our region. CUF is changing and remodelling under Rob's leadership. So I am keen to ask him what kindness means to him as he leads this work:

> I think kindness is connected deeply to the questions, 'What does it mean to be graceful? What does it mean to be merciful? What does it mean to be a disciple?' For me to thrive as a Christian, there's something about 'I need the other to thrive', and therefore recognizing that there is a need for culture-setting which enables the other to thrive, and what are the best ways in which we can do that in terms of setting up a culture or a posture of kindness.

Rob views his role as CEO and bishop as 'being Barnabas',[5] 'being the encourager'. He takes this role seriously as he sets the culture. He explains:

> Our Christian life is about being rooted in God's love, and being rooted in God's hopes and desires, and so therefore we're joining in with God on the mission of God. It is in God's inherent nature, it seems to me, in Jesus, for kindness.

I am particularly interested in how a culture of kindness can be nurtured in a dispersed organization such as CUF, which is dependent on its network for so much of its operational capacity. Rob places a high value on the journey of faith and the prayers of the saints, 'the great cloud of witnesses'[6] who shape our collective Christian life. He describes a 'brutal kindness' that is present in their ministry. He cites the case of Laurence the Deacon[7] who, before his cruel death, handed out all the wealth to the most 'marginalized in society, the widows and the poor, and went beyond himself when it could have been easier, and perhaps a kind thing, to save himself by handling the treasures more politically – this is what I mean by brutal kindness'.

Choosing kindness – the kindness of others over your own cause – can be a brutal or costly choice that perhaps is the gift of the privileged and powerful. I wonder if using privilege wisely and for the common good is a kindness that extends beyond an individual and has the potential to impact more than one person or group. In many ways this is the work of CUF – encouraging the Church of England to use its privilege as the Established Church in England, to extend itself to a kindness that is more than its legal obligations or its social intentions. Perhaps even acting against its own interests and handing out the treasures to the marginalized and the left behind. This is more than charity or good stewardship: this is an extension of kindness that is costly and, in Rob's terms, brutally self-sacrificing. I certainly see that sacrifice at the rock face, in our parishes and neighbourhoods. Many are the modern saints who give up a great deal to respond to human need and challenge unjust structures.

24

When to forgive

Ravi Holy, priest, comedian and founder of Heal for Life

29 September 2025

> Self-compassion can put you in a position where you have the energy to treat people kindly. It's rather like the instruction you get on planes that you should put your own oxygen mask on first, before helping others. You're better able to assist someone else if you're not worrying about yourself.
>
> *Claudia Hammond*[1]

Ravi Holy is Rector of Wye in Kent and a stand-up comedian. Ravi was a punk and went to public school; he loves music, popular culture and film. The first time I met Ravi he was visiting our theological college to give us a talk on universalism based on his undergraduate theology degree thesis.[2] Though I wasn't wholly convinced of his argument, I was intrigued – particularly as he offered an alternative to what can be considered the 'cruel doctrine of penal substitution'. The second time I met Ravi I was on retreat and he and his two clergy friends turned up for their annual retreat. The 'Three Amigos', as they are known, share a love of film and Jesus, and their company was a great tonic for my weary prayers that day. The third time I met Ravi he stayed at our house as he had a stand-up comedy gig at a local comedy club. I went to the gig – he was funny.

Ravi is the founder of Heal for Life,[3] a charity for survivors of childhood trauma and abuse. The following conversation contains some references to Ravi's abuse, about forgiveness and withholding forgiveness. If these are concerns that might trigger difficult things for you, if you choose to read this reflection, please be gentle with yourself.

> If you've ever been my friend, then you're always my friend. It's never gonna be me that ends it. I suppose that's something I quite like about myself. I think that's a good quality. I also think that that's what God's like. And, as you know, theologically, I'm a universalist, because it seems obvious to me that if I feel like that about people, how much more must God feel? I mean, however kind I am, God must be kinder. And therefore, if I never give up on anyone, how much more must that be the case for God.

Ravi has lived experience as a survivor of abuse, which led him to found a charity that works with small groups of survivors in a residential environment. I ask Ravi about this work and how the model that has been developed enables survivors to explore kindness and forgiveness:

> I am trying to link kindness with my abuse survivor charity work – this is a secular charity and it offers a therapeutic model. I am thinking about one of the songs that we use in my retreats for survivors – it's a song written by a survivor called 'My Brave Heart'. It's a song sung to the brave survivor within – no matter what life throws at you, you keep getting up and carrying on, 'my brave heart'. There's a line about: when someone needs forgiving, you're the first to get in line. I think that's a positive thing, never writing people off, always being willing to give people a second chance.
>
> I'm very wary to talk about forgiveness. I never really talk about forgiveness in the context of survivors, because raising the issue of forgiveness with survivors of abuse is kind of abusive. Ironically, having said that, the only people I have cut out of my life are my own parents, who were my primary abusers. I haven't had any contact with them for 14 years. And my only regret, really, is that I hadn't made that decision about 20 years earlier, which would have saved me a lot of heartache. It was because I was trying to be a good Christian and forgive, so I kept banging my head against that particular brick wall.

My conversation with Ravi led me to consider when it is appropriate to forgive and when we might withhold forgiveness. Perhaps we have to leave some things with the law. Maybe they are left with God. Discerning the place of kindness in this is important. In Ravi's case he eventually discerned that forgiving his parents was ultimately not an act of self-kindness. I can see this has been a hard road and a tough decision to make. But that's where kindness finds him now.

If you feel you need support to process any form of abuse, please do not feel alone. There are people who can support you. Find a Helpline[4] *has a comprehensive list of various appropriate support networks. Your local church safeguarding officer, diocesan safeguarding team, the police or social services all know what to do.*

25

Treat people with kindness

Charlotte Gale, priest and author

27 September 2025

> The Kindness Economy is a movement for how consumer culture needs (and wants) to change. The landscape of how people buy, sell, make and live has to change. We need social progress to go hand in hand with commerce.
>
> *Mary Portas*[1]

Charlotte Gale is a priest in the Church of England, she and her partner Naomi Nixon lead St Clare's, an inclusive missional community based at Coventry Cathedral. St Clare's is also a shop tucked between the old and new cathedral run as an ethical social business.[2]

Given our shared interests in ethical business, social justice, mission and cathedral ministry, Charlotte and I are surprised we haven't ever met before. As we begin to talk it feels as though we have shared many an hour ruminating and setting the world to rights. I have read Charlotte's book, *Simple, Generous, Open: Mission and renewal in the progressive church*[3] so I am aware of the struggles she and Naomi have faced to keep their ministries and the community alive. Their story is a story of survival and courage, and Charlotte speaks about how progressive church can be a place for brave mission that reaches out to those who struggle to find a place in the mainstream – 'younger folks, socially awkward folks, people with neurodiversity, and queer people'. Charlotte tells me that St Clare's wants to reach out to those who have been made to feel 'unwelcome or excluded or like they don't just quite fit in in life, to feel like they are treasured and loved and part of a community'. The shop is crucial to the kindness of St Clare's and Charlotte clearly thrives there:

> I've always loved working in shops. When I was a teenager, I did shops. I worked in every shop in the village which I grew up in. Also, Naomi's dad ran an independent bookshop for some years, so we felt like we knew about it. And I think business does sound hard on one level, but shops are extraordinary places of kindness. I think that in small shops, certainly, that kindness is still an important part of a thriving business. St Clare's has three values, the simple, generous and open.

I love the idea that shops can be places of kindness. Perhaps it is harder to find this in the big chain experience but in the small, local businesses I can see that this will be a vital part of their connection with people. It's about seeing people not just as customers but also as individuals who share similar values and interests. The rise of the social business and cooperative movement has brought fresh interest in the social economy. In countries such as South Korea[4] and Spain[5] the social economy is booming. Organizations such as Global Social Economic Forum[6] and Power to Change[7] are working to enable social businesses to find a legitimate place in the complex world of economics.

In the case of St Clare's their commitment to kindness expends to their ethical approach:

> Most of our stock is fair trade, we carbon offset, and when people come in, you know, I spend an enormous amount of time just chatting to people, being kind to the people who come in, and if someone wants to exchange something, I just exchange it, I don't ask any questions, I don't demand a receipt. [We] try hard to be as generous and kind in our dealings as we can.

It feels right that this community is based in Coventry; a place of peace and justice, tucked in the space between the old and new cathedral that rose out of the ashes of the Second World War. I ask Charlotte about the importance of this place as a liminal space of kindness:

> I think at Coventry, of course, we've got the perfect example of that. The Provost, the day after the cathedral is destroyed, stands in the ruins and says, 'Father, forgive.' He doesn't say, 'Father, forgive them.' He acknowledges that war is caused very rarely in a vacuum. I think the reason that we were able to rebuild after the Second World War in such an extraordinary and effective way in terms of our relationship with Europe, was in part, because of his words. What came from that was a desire to make friends. The first twinning came out of that with

> Dresden, with an acknowledgement that we have done awful things to each other. Reconciliation required a humility that we've all failed, and to do justice we also need kindness and humility.

This connection with the old and new vision for reconciliation, justice, kindness and humility is what sets St Clare's apart. A kind shop that creates community for those who are seeking refuge from an unkind world.

26

Prioritizing the soul

Eve Poole, writer and expert on leadership, and Executive Chair of Woodard Schools

29 September 2025

> The problem is, the soul is not a knowable item and if we stare at it for long enough, it does not look like a perfect form: all we see is junk code.
>
> *Eve Poole*[1]

Eve Poole[2] and I are excellent sparring partners, we can talk about almost anything and find joy in mashing up the most obscure of subjects including robots, economics, education and Jesus. Her latest book *Robot Souls: Programming in humanity* was the subject of the Liverpool Cathedral Social Justice Micah Lecture in 2024. The programming of humanity into AI and the rise of its use in everyday life is of particular interest to Eve, so it is not surprising that we quickly move our conversation on to the importance of treating the human soul with kindness:

> I would hope that kindness is being able to see into someone's eyes, into the windows of their soul, listen gently, and be able to treat the soul. So, this is where I think Cure of Souls is such a lovely expression, and I don't think it is what a lot of clergy do, but I think it is what we're supposed to be doing – tending to the soul. But being alive to the fact that the soul is encased in a person who has had to develop personality in order to flourish in the world they find themselves in. And there may be a whole host of complicated negotiations they've had to enter into to be able to survive that, and it is unkind to strip that back, and it would be incredibly unkind to name it or challenge it if that's not the contract you have with the person. But it is about trying to keep the soul in mind and contextualize that within whatever you're reading about the kind

> of processes that you've developed of coping, so that you can prioritize their soul but take account of their personality as well.

There is something profoundly gentle and kind about what Eve is proposing here. The prioritizing of the soul (your own or another's) is a deeply kind act, and placing the flourishing of what makes us human as a primary extends kindness beyond material benefit to a spiritual realm. This kindness is spiritual and holy. Eve identifies her husband and father as two people who possess this soul kindness, men who 'truly listen and hear somebody else's soul. Who could be on the wavelength, be available to be on that wavelength.' I wonder if Eve thinks she has inherited any of her father's soul kindness:

> I'm very bad at the whole seeing Christ in everyone, but I try to recognize that we're all ensouled. And if you can connect at a soul level, then everything will become clear, and everything will be as it should be. And I suppose I'm always trying to reach out to that soul in a person. And I suppose I've given up very rarely on people, but if I think about people I've given up on, it's because I can't get to their soul, and I'm not sure they even have one. I mean, obviously existentially, I don't believe that, but it's so locked away that I don't think that conversation is possible.

I am intrigued as to whether this practice of soul kindness can be applied to systems or processes. Eve offered her work as Church of England Third Estates Commissioner as an example of the way in which she attempted to infuse kindness into the governance review of cathedrals:

> I really believe in the cathedrals, and I was very worried about the kind of policy direction of travel, which was about starving them of resource and importance. I think the cathedrals themselves are kind, because they are available to anybody who wants to come searching and seeking. They're a place of connection for soul, magnets for kindness. Not always institutionally, but in terms of what the gesture is. I thought, I need to hold the space open for the cathedrals to breathe.
>
> So I entered into a spirit of listening more and deliberately holding my hypotheses incredibly gently. I did have a view that they needed to report to the Charity Commission as a sort of matter of principle, because that was the key change, and if we weren't doing that, there was no point. But other than that, whether it was the consultation I did with deans at St George's, whether it was the fringe meetings at Synod, whether it was the conversations in Parliament, conversations in Synod

itself ... With all the communities, and particularly in the revision committee, it was about listening really hard to what the cathedrals felt needed to be said, and the things that they were worrying about, and the things they felt would be more life-giving. It doesn't look like a kind measure, it looks like a boring piece of legislation, but there was a lot of kindness behind it.

So, for instance, there was a panic at one point that the administrators weren't getting enough traction, and they weren't getting enough credit for the fact that they run a lot of the big cathedrals, and there was a huge amount of consternation about that, so we very deliberately built a bit of wording in the measure drawing on gifts of the Spirit, about administration being a gift of the Spirit, to make it clear that we felt administration was crucial theologically. There was also a sunset clause for those members of cathedral chapters who were there as Chief Executive types, and under the new measure wouldn't keep their role on chapter, but it would have been so cruel not to find a bridge through that for them. So I suppose it was an exercise in corporate kindness in the way you don't often see, because people tend to come in bish-bash-bosh. And I was very deliberately trying to hold the ring for there to be that space for cathedrals to self-determine in a way that they hadn't really felt listened to or able to do and be. And so, some of the lobbying for money and different sorts of delegations and help was trying to be kind, trying to let the souls of the cathedrals breathe.

As a member of a cathedral chapter that has gone through the process of adapting to the Cathedral Measure 2021,[3] I appreciate the time spent listening and laying the ground for the implementation as well as the structures that have been put in place. I *can* see and I feel the kindness in the new architecture of governance. Our cathedrals are places where people can open their souls and catch a breath. Many cathedrals are in danger of losing their soul space under the financial pressure, to be venues more often than places of worship where people can come and breathe. I pray we can continue to enable our cathedrals as places where we can open our heart and soul to what it means to be human, to be made in the image of God, and to be free to breathe deeply.

27

Mutuality

Sam Wells, vicar, writer, broadcaster

29 September 2025

> I'd like to live in a world where the greatest thing you could say about a person is that they were kind.
>
> *Claudia Hammond*[1]

There is a power in finding kindness in another person and discovering that there is an affinity in your connection. You see something in the other person that resonates and connects with your own struggles and enables you to understand the work God has been doing in your own life. It changes you and sets you off on a new path. This is what happens when Simon/Peter meets Cornelius and Cornelius meets Simon/Peter.[2] They do not know it until they meet, but they have been waiting for each other ... and their mutuality was to change not only their lives but the direction of God's mission to the world.

Sam Wells has been vicar at St Martin-in-the-Fields[3] since 2012; he is a writer, broadcaster and social commentator. Sam and I have been talking about kindness for 20 minutes before he mentions the passage from Acts 10.24–33. At this point our connection to kindness intensifies and the conversation takes a fresh direction.

> With the Peter and Cornelius story what intrigues me is, whose territory are we on? It's Israel, so you think it's Jewish territory, but obviously it's occupied by the Romans, so it's Cornelius' territory. Cornelius calls Peter to his house. So that's his territory. But Peter is the one who decides whether you can be a Christian or not, so it's his territory. That's quite intriguing. There's a mutuality of kindness in that story: that's why I coined the term *guestability*. Part of this conversation about kindness is about territory, and the unspoken, or usually unstated, power

assumptions and the context of kindness, which can qualify it in significant ways.

Sam continues:

> Certainly, in Jesus' ministry, his response to hospitality is the kind of demanding of hospitality from Zacchaeus and lots of stories about territory with Jesus, and of course, if we think of Jesus as the second Person in the Trinity, the whole world is his. And yet, as the beginning of John's Gospel puts it, the world received him not. So there's a lot of ambiguity. His first teaching to his disciples is quite brutal about receiving or not receiving hospitality.

Sam has defined kindness as a 'supererogatory act of grace beyond the expected, beyond the social norm, beyond the family. So, you can see Jesus, as that is almost a definition of his ministry.' Jesus has set the bar for how kindness should be enacted and experienced. Sam refers to Richard and Christopher Hay's book *The Widening of God's Mercy*[4] in which they explore the ever-widening reach of the mercy of God out into the world. 'The whole Bible from Abraham onwards, is a story of the ever-widening of God's mercy, and therefore an ever-expanding circle of kindness.'

> My only problem with that is it has a centre and a periphery, and it can position the Church as benevolently reaching out to those it perceives to be marginal – which is still a bit patronizing and self-satisfied. But it's a lot better than most of the things it's replacing. My most recent book, *Constructing an Incarnational Theology*,[5] is really saying we have made a mistake by assuming Jesus came to fix the Fall. Instead, Jesus was coming anyway. Jesus was the fundamental, foundational, definitive embodiment of God's primordial desire to be with us before the foundation of the world, as several passages in the New Testament put it.

In this sense the kindness Sam is describing is mutual: God reaches out to humanity in the person of Jesus and as a result we are brought back into the familial loving-kindness that was there at the beginning of time. The ever-widening of God's mercy is extending this loving-kindness exponentially – it cannot be contained, and its edges should not be limited. Kindness is a 'prophetic action' that by its very being is an act of justice and reconciliation and a gift from God. 'It is all about relationships' and connection – with each other and with our God.

28

Clear is kind

Kate Wharton, vicar, trustee of Single Friendly Church

29 September 2025

> It's simple but transformative: Clear is kind. Unclear is unkind.
>
> I first heard this saying two decades ago in a 12-step meeting, but I was on slogan overload at the time and didn't even think about it again until I saw the data about how most of us avoid clarity because we tell ourselves that we're being kind, when what we're actually doing is being unkind and unfair.
>
> Feeding people half-truths or bullshit to make them feel better (which is almost always about making ourselves feel more comfortable) is unkind.
>
> *Brene Brown*[1]

Being kind might seem easy, but as we lead into our conversation Kate reminds me that 'it's actually deep and ... difficult and risky'. Kate Wharton is Vicar of St Bartholomew's Church in Roby, Liverpool;[2] she is a writer and member of the Church of England General Synod. She has written extensively about singleness[3] and is a trustee of Single Friendly Church.[4] Kate and I have been part of some difficult conversations, but I have always found her kind – she listens and is unafraid to offer her perspective. We don't always agree on certain issues, but we remain committed to each other's well-being.

Kate is the Prolocutor of the Lower House of the Convocation of York, which means she represents and speaks for me and all the other Church of England clergy in the North. So I am interested in how Kate navigates this responsibility with kindness. She explains that it is vital to her that it maintains relationships with people that may not share her views. She offers an example:

> For me, as someone who holds the particular sort of theological view around sexuality, for instance, one of the real frustrations to me is that other people who hold a similar viewpoint to me, I then experience or observe them speaking in ways that are – you can debate whether or not they're unkind – but they're certainly unhelpful. So, it's one of the things that's really mattered to me at Synod, that I am going to speak clearly about what I believe, but I always want to do that kindly. For me, there are a few ways in which that works out. One way is that I will always try to maintain personal relationships with people and talk directly to people as well, because otherwise how are they going to experience what I say publicly if I haven't also got a relationship with them? There's something about 'present your opponent's position generously'. Try and present it as well as possible, almost as if you're arguing for it, see the good points in it. And then just remember that they are human, we're brothers and sisters.

Kate acknowledges that this may seem basic manners and Christian ethics but suggests that it isn't always what she sees and hears from people in Synod. She is aware that the way Synod debates isn't always kind; so, I ask her why she thinks our leadership slips into these confrontational debates:

> Anybody who serves on Archbishops' Council with me currently would tell you that my mantra, it's even made it into the Code of Conduct that I've just written for Archbishops' Council, is the Brene Brown phrase about 'clear is kind, unclear is unkind'. I just say that all the time, because I think so often that's one of the problems that lies behind all of this, because we're trying to be nice, we end up being unkind, because we're unclear. I spoke to the College of Bishops a couple of weeks ago. I was asked to do a workshop on well-being, and what clergy often say to me is, 'We just wish they'd just tell us.' You know, whatever it might be, whether it's about jobs, or about housing, whatever it might be – just be clear.

It is possible that leaders don't always have the clarity to offer those they lead. Perhaps we are asking too much of our leaders. It is possible that the sort of clarity we need is a recognition that our leaders are also searching and wrestling with contested ideas in challenging situations. I also suspect that many who speak publicly in places such as Synod may be driven by a desire to win rather than *debate*. Perhaps insecurity drives desperation for certainty rather than an acceptance that control is not ours to determine. It might be possible that in these contested times it is best to keep talking and listening, better to create space for the other rather than draw a circle around our own dominion. Lengthen the table.[5] Speak to the crowd about kindness, grace and abundance, feed the thousands instead of sending them home hungry.[6]

29

Obstinate kindness

Paula Gooder, Canon Chancellor, St Paul's Cathedral

30 September 2025

> I believe in a world ... where we value kindness as the most important and meaningful resource we have available to us, and we treat it with the reverence, ritual, and relentless exercise that it's due. I believe in a world where thoughtful and ongoing practice of kindness is the number one way we measure our collective and individual successes.
>
> *Houston Kraft*[1]

Paula Gooder[2] is Chancellor at St Paul's Cathedral; she is a writer, academic and theologian. Paula begins our kindness conversation by describing kindness as both an attitude and an action; an attitude of 'thinking positively, thinking well of people', and an action in that you 'act seeking the best for other people, you act expecting the best from other people'. She adds that 'kindness overlaps a little bit with naivety, but kind of deliberate naivety'. Yes, I can see that for many of us kindness is a hopeful action that almost innocently projects goodness into challenging situations. Perhaps this is what indomitable people do when they are determined that things shouldn't be as horrible as they seem; when faced with cruel people they resolutely refuse to bat back a curveball of meanness – what Paula describes as obstinate kindness. Paula refers to Jesus' parable of the widow who never gave up:[3]

> I think it's really rather lovely, because Jesus introduces it by saying he taught them a parable about praying and never giving up. I think there is something about kindness, about kind of *obstinate kindness*, when you are determinedly kind, even though the evidence around you suggests that that's a bad idea.

People who insist on kindness against the odds are courageous and seekers of justice. They choose kindness despite everything that their experience tells them is sensible. Paula continues to explain:

> You get to a stage in life where you've ended up suffering a whole load of things, and people have been really quite unkind to you, but deliberately choosing to be naive, and say, well, perhaps in this instance it won't be like that. Another word that pops into mind is hope, that kind of theological hope and not kind of general hope.

Is this the hope that Paul has when he speaks about kindness in his letters? In Colossians 3 when he tells the church to 'clothe yourselves with compassion, kindness, humility, meekness, and patience'?[4] Or when he tells the Ephesian church to be kind to one another[5] and forgive, or that kindness is a fundamental expression of love when the church in Corinth[6] are on the edge of giving up on love? And the church in Rome who are in a muddle about what makes people turn their lives around and Paul explains that it is God's kindness that is the transforming power that leads to repentance?[7] All this hope from Paul came while he is in chains. He talks about kind Barnabas and needing Timothy to minister in Troy. What Paula points out is that kindness is a vital part of Paul's teaching to the early Church. It is countercultural in a similar way to now, in that dominant Greco-Roman culture was self-absorbed, driven by capital and empire-focused. Kindness and compassion cuts through this and it offers an alternative kingdom vision of justice and peace. This vision of countercultural kindness requires hope, faith and love to survive.[8]

Paula contends that this kindness also requires consistency as well as determination – seeking 'the best for a person and for the whole'. Our conversation segways into a debate about the common good and whether this side of the glory (my term) or eschaton (Paula's more scholarly term) we will be able to do this with any success:

> What pops into my mind and, when I'm talking about common good, is, maybe the best we can hope for in this time is the common good enough. What Paul recognizes is that the end of all times, when God is fully with people, loving-kindness is the expression that it is possible to have everywhere and always. In those times, loving-kindness will be complete. There is no oppression, no sorrow, no sighing, all of those things are gone. But what we can do now is to recognize that Jesus' resurrection has brought in glimmers of it.

What we can hope for are glimmers of glory and snapshots of obstinate kindness.

30

Peace of mind

Andrew Rumsey, Bishop of Ramsbury, writer and musician

6 October 2025

> The kind of kindness we need today acknowledges that a compassionate world is not a passive by-product of hope, but an active, daily, resilient battle that is hard-won.
>
> *Houston Kraft*[1]

Everyone that has taken part in this project has been identified either by me or someone else as being a kind person. One of the questions I have asked participants is why they think this has been recognized in them. Almost without fail this question embarrasses or makes the person interviewed visibly squirm. For many, the thought of being kind lightens their demeanour, they brighten and there is a hint of pleasure in the possibility that someone thinks they are kind. This is very much the case with Andrew.

I ask Andrew what he thinks kindness is and why it has made him so uncomfortable to be considered kind:

> It begins for me in a sense of conscious weakness. And I do think, therefore, it is linked to humility. Not that one would ever refer to oneself in that way. I was surprised and pleased to be sought out about this theme. Kindness begins with a sense of my own limitation. And how much I want and need others' kindness. A sense of conscious weakness, but also, awareness of lack of confidence. If I'm honest, there are vast areas of life and work and human engagement, relationship, and everything, where we find ourselves up against our own limitations. And where our capacity is not sufficient. I do think that kindness begins, for me, in a sense, in self-awareness and consciousness of my own weakness.

I am intrigued by this admission of weakness but also that, for Andrew, kindness emerges from a place of humility. Kindness takes on a particular strength when it comes from a place of modesty. It is hard to tag yourself as a kind person, but it feels good to tag someone else as such. One of the joys of this project is being able to tell people they are kind and see the pleasure that has brought.

Andrew loves telling me about the kindness of his children – particularly his eldest daughter, whom he describes as 'luminous with kindness, and everybody sees it in her, and it's a beautiful thing'. While he is clearly proud, he is also aware of the necessity for her to 'work out the cost of it and try to moderate it, and not let it exhaust her, and make space for what she needs and wants'.

Family kindness is something Andrew treasures and he tells me about his father, Philip Rumsey:

> I do want to mention my dad, because my late father was the kind of wellspring for all of this (familial kindness). He died a long time ago, nearly 30 years ago, a couple of months before I was ordained. He was a parish priest, and my principal role model in everything. He had a very gentle, kind, local ministry which was the example of my life, really. I measure everything against that. We had an unusually close relationship, I would say. So it was a bizarre and difficult thing to be launched into ministry without him.

I can see that people – Andrew's people – are important to him. I also appreciate that as deacon, priest and now bishop that extension of family and the responsibility of sharing cure of souls is important to him. Of equal importance is a sense of place, of belonging:

> The ethic of the kingdom must be practised, and places formed – when God and community and land integrate. So I think there's something around the radical power of kindness in the forming of community and the way in which local pastoral ministry is non-sectarian.
>
> I fear a drift towards sectarian ideology in the Church, and I think the last ten years have seen the Church become more sectarian in its default culture. For all sorts of reasons, but I don't like it. And the more we drift in that direction, the less I recognize the Church that I love. I resist sectarianism.

I share Andrew's concern that as we divide, we become less able to serve our communities and represent diversity in prayer and sacrament in the places we are called to as priests. The privilege of the Established Church is the cure of souls for all in our parishes, and this means praying for all people in that place – without distinction. I am an Anglican because I strive to belong to a church that is kind in the face of distinction and diversity. The Church of England serves from the local to the centre, from parish to diocese to nation.

> How does the kingdom of God grow? If you listen to the teaching of Jesus, you know, it's a seed growing quietly.

31

The forgotten gift

Paul Northup, Creative Director, Greenbelt festival

7 October 2025

Greenbelt Festival is somewhere artistry meets activism, where the political meets the practical. We're somewhere to come together once a year, where we're as likely to dream up a better world as we are to dance and debate, to pray and to party.

We were founded a long time ago by a bunch of misfits in a field. We're still in a field. And we're still somewhere that welcomes anyone and everyone.

Greenbelt Festival[1]

Paul Northup is the gentle, unassuming Creative Director of Greenbelt festival. Greenbelt has become more than the once-a-year experience of hanging out in a field with Christians, activists, artists and thinkers. Greenbelt has grown generations of creative, faithful people who live connected and challenging lives – pushing their faith and asking questions of their governments and churches. If you haven't already seen the Greenbelt Manifesto,[2] then it's worth a read.

As our conversation begins, I ask Paul how he defines kindness:

I think it's an attitude, an approach; I think it can be a disposition, sort of like a character. I think you only get to that being a disposition or a character trait by adopting an attitude and an approach and a commitment to kindness. The thing that would underline all of those things I've said is that, at the end of the day, it's a practice, it's something you can actually get better at, and that you have to maintain. It's a gift that's given, but it's a gift that needs nourishing and treasuring in order for it to give back, and to be the 'gift that keeps on giving'.

> Kindness has such a profound effect on you when you encounter it. I want to try and emulate that. It feels like a *forgotten gift*. It's like something we just slightly take for granted. It feels like culturally or politically, even spiritually, we've stopped paying attention to kindness.

Forgetting kindness is perhaps the reason why there is a harsh tone in our critical encounters and political debates. Perhaps this is why culture feels exhausting and so much of our society fractured. That golden thread of 'we are doing this stuff so we can build a better world' has got tarnished and worn by a constant barrage of brutality. What if all our critical discourse was framed by the pursuit of kindness? That would be transformational. In some ways this is what Greenbelt attempts to do – to unwrap the forgotten gift of kindness and create an environment where human flourishing is primary. Paul explains:

> Each of us can try and practise kindness as best we're able and form it into a habit: when you then commit yourselves and belong to others and live in community with others who are attempting to model that same form of kindness. Together it can start to become what might look like justice: you can walk humbly, you can love kindness and try and model it in your own life, but I think that to really do justice you need to do that with others. That's what I've found in Greenbelt. Over my years of going to it and being involved in it, I found, on the one hand, people, individuals who are Christ-like, kind. But I've also found a body of people who are the most brave and prophetic when it comes to trying to live justly and challenge injustice. So, I found both those things alongside each other.

There is something so glorious in finding people to collaborate with – co-conspirators for justice and kindness. And I have met many at Greenbelt. Paul sums this up: 'There is something about being gathered, and about what can happen in the gathered space, in the community, that is so much more transformational than expected.'

32

The searing truth

David Porter, former Chief of Staff to the Archbishop of Canterbury

7 October 2025

All have sinned and fallen short of the glory of God.
The hatred which divides nation from nation, race from race, class from class,
Father, forgive.
The covetous desires of people and nations to possess what is not their own,
Father, forgive.
The greed which exploits the work of human hands and lays waste the earth,
Father, forgive.
Our envy of the welfare and happiness of others,
Father, forgive.
Our indifference to the plight of the imprisoned, the homeless, the refugee,
Father, forgive.
The lust which dishonours the bodies of men, women and children,
Father, forgive.
The pride which leads us to trust in ourselves and not in God,
Father, forgive.
Be kind to one another, tender-hearted, forgiving one another, as God in Christ forgave you.

Coventry Cathedral Litany of Reconciliation[1]

David Porter is sitting in his study relaxed and content in his retirement, enjoying his first coffee of the day. My experience of David is that he is a truth-teller, a man of clarity and straight talking. I spent some time with him in 2019 in Belfast, meeting people who have been involved in creating and holding peace in the island of Ireland. The visit was hosted by Archbishop Justin Welby and led by David, who was then the Archbishop's Chief of Staff. We heard uncomfortable truths and stories of hope and despair during our time together. David held the space firmly but gently as we were introduced to his 'friends'. So our kindness conversation begins with an observation about the importance of kindness in truth-telling:

> It requires searing truths to be told in the context of kindness. As, if you try to tell the truths without the kindness, rooted in the grace, then truths and justice become a sharp, double-edged sword. It rips communities and peoples apart.

I ask David how he defines kindness. He replies:

> Kindness for me is simply the ability to see the humanity of the other. And to treat them as a fully human person, how you would want to be treated. So sometimes kindness is strong. It's about confronting the person in front of you. Sometimes kindness is about support – kindness is always about unquestioning support of the person but not necessarily support for what they do. To me, it's not a soppy feeling, it's an action. It's an attitude.

David has a robust and self-assured approach to kindness. There is no messing about with overindulgent feelings of niceness – this kindness is confident. The confidence is found in the person of Jesus 'because of what we've experienced from God. God in Christ has entered our world not to condemn us, but to save us, and empathizes with us and knows our weaknesses, and is still there for us.' David has this faithful undefended assurance that kindness, as a fruit of the Spirit, is a searing truth that is transformational.

During our conversation we touch on some difficult subjects: the way that sexual abuse cases have been handled by the Church of England, the violence in Gaza, immigration, the resignation of Justin Welby, the staff at Lambeth Palace. In all these concerns David argues that there are no straightforward narratives – that to simplify these issues into a single account or a one-sided story would be disingenuous. David insists, 'Kindness is about being truthful about the complexity.' I ask David, how might we reveal the complexity of a situation? 'A commitment to do that through hard telling and honest remembering is, to me, being kind.'

33

A bridge

Isabelle Hamley, Principal, Ridley Hall, Cambridge

7 October 2025

> To live well, we must be able to imaginatively identify with other people and allow them to identify with us. Unkindness involves a failure of the imaginative so acute that it threatens not just our happiness but our sanity. Caring for others ... is what makes us fully human.
>
> *Adam Philips and Barbara Taylor*[1]

Isabelle and I focus our conversation on the ability of kindness to transform the way we speak about the difficult issues we face as a church community and as social humans in complex relationships. We discuss the possibility that kindness can create a connection with someone that doesn't share your world view, political or theological position:

> I've seen people from equally opposite angles who disagree, but have such profound kindness towards the other that somehow it creates a bridge where it feels like there should be no bridge. This has become important to me as how we do ministry, and an encouragement that the end doesn't justify the means. It doesn't matter what your goal is. You can apply it to lots of things, not just contentious debates, but I've seen people who care so much about mission or evangelism but in the process forget to be kind to the people that are around them, to the people that God has already given them to look after, like in a parish. Well, OK, you might want to care for those people who aren't in your parish yet, or who don't come to church yet, but if in the process you're unkind to your existing congregation, what does that say about what it is you want to achieve in terms of mission and evangelism anyway?

I agree that kindness can be a bridge to connect us as much as an unkindness can create insurmountable boundaries that divide. I wonder, if achievements are at the cost of kindness, how can they be justified? Isabelle continues:

> Vision and strategy are big buzzwords in the Church of England at the moment, and there's part of me that's slightly more interested in values. What kind of people are we, because if we don't pay attention to values and character, I think our strategy ... well, it's the Corinthians 13 thing, if you don't have love, you're a clanging cymbal, and it will all be in vain, and I think kindness is an aspect of love. If we don't have love and kindness, a lot of our big projects and big ideas are just ... pointless.

I am encouraged to hear Isabelle, as principal of a theological college, speaking about values and character. I heard this same point made by Michael Leyden, principal of Emmauel Theological College. These are theological educators who equip their ordinands not just to manage projects and inspire new missional initiatives but also to appreciate the task of nurturing what already exists in worshipping communities and enable all to flourish.

Isabelle tells a story that illustrates her point beautifully:

> I was at the Lambeth Conference and there was a contested space around sexuality. But at the final Eucharist it just so happened that a bishop who was gay and partnered from the US was sitting next to a bishop from a very conservative province in the Global South who had been told by his Archbishop he was not allowed to take communion. So the bishop from the US went up to communion and brought back his wafer, sat down at his seat, back in the congregation, split his wafer, and shared it with the Global South bishop next to him. And they shared communion together. That was incredible. I think, for me, that was the most salient image of the Lambeth Conference I've seen. I saw again and again people showing kindness to each other, despite very deep division. And when something like that happens, you can't go back to a polarized position, because something has happened at a human level that meant that you've encountered each other. It just transformed something. It is transformational on all sides. It is about people choosing to honour the other person as a person first and to take seriously the fact that no one knows what it's like to be this other person. There was miracle in the fact that one bishop chose to bring

back his wafer, and there was miracle in the fact that the other bishop chose to accept it.

Kindness is miraculous and transformational, a bridge and a bond-maker. It changes lives because it puts humanity before obligation. I am going to be kind because I love you, and love and kindness is more important than anything else.

34

Collective kindness

Chris Howson, university chaplain

10 October 2025

> How lovely to think that no one need wait a moment, we can start now, start slowly changing the world! How lovely that everyone, great and small, can make their contribution toward introducing justice straightaway ... And you can always, always give something, even if it is only kindness!
>
> *Anne Frank*[1]

Chris Howson was one of my brother's friends when growing up. My brother Howard became a probation officer; Chris became the Church of England chaplain at Sunderland University – they both grew up to be kind. Chris values 'collective kindness', a kindness that is 'inclusive and contagious':

> Kindness means people feeling welcomed and loved and cherished where they are, whether they're a stranger or known to people. Kindness is a kind of gentleness with the human soul. You see kindness explode in the camaraderie of a football pitch and kids playing with their families, and a church which is genuinely inclusive and welcoming of people. Kindness makes people feel valued and loved.

I wonder what sort of kindness might emerge within an institution such as a university. Chris explains:

> I think churches and universities need to be aware of that, not just rely on the one or two obviously lovely, kind people around, but that you can encourage a kind of collective kindness. Which is beautiful when you see it enacted.

> There's a spirit of listening, of being non-judgemental. A spirit of hopefulness about how the world can be. I think individuals can embody it, and I think kindness can be contagious.

The idea of an institution being able to develop a collective kindness interests me. Is this something led from the centre or emerging from the margins, I wonder? Chris suggests that in his experience it's the ordinary members of a community that lead kindness.

> We have one or two older women in our congregation I would instantly describe as kind. I think Gillian is a kind, prayerful person, and a welcoming person, and wanting-to-help person. And I think her kindness is contagious.

As a city of sanctuary, Sunderland has a reputation as being kind to the stranger – welcoming refugees and asylum seekers. This has been hard fought for by people like Chris, as well as his students and congregation. This commitment has emerged from the people of the city, and their leaders have taken this into legislation. However, the rise of Reform in the area is challenging this commitment. Chris fears an erosion of a visible collective kindness. 'Societies can quickly become unkind, and post-pandemic Britain has gone in a direction that we never thought it would. The world seems to have shifted.'

Chris wants us to be realistic about how hard society might become if we allow the erosion of human rights and for kindness to be lost:

> In the future, because we're going to go through an unkind period, I think, we have to be realistic about that and not feel that that's the end of the show. Imagine living in Nazi Germany in the 1930s. Imagine seeing the slipping of human rights, and the slipping of kindness going on then. Imagine living through the debt crisis in Latin America, or the far-right dictatorships of the '60s, '70s, '80s and '90s – it must have felt that you'd never get kindness back, and yet it does come back, because it's instilled in our human DNA. In what God wants us to be.

Losing our human rights, normalizing racism and misogyny, allowing nihilism to dominate and reactionary dogma to flourish – this is a real possibility, particularly if the anchor institutions[2] such as universities, churches (and other faith groups), health-care providers and the third sector do not stand up and resist. It is in these areas of our societies that we see kindness flourishing and it is in these spaces that we need to invest

– not simply financial investment but also cultural investment. These are the places ordinary Christians and people of faith need to inhabit. If we want to see collective kindness blossom, we must feed it, enable it to spread like a glorious contagion.

35

Interrupting kindness

Ayla Lepine, art historian and priest

13 October 2025

> For all things come from you, and of your own have we given you.
>
> *Chronicles 29.14*

Ayla Lepine is Associate Rector at St James's, Piccadilly;[1] she is an academic, art historian, theologian and author. If you follow Ayla on social media, you will discover rich and varied postings about art, social justice and culture. I love listening to Ayla speak about art, and recently we had the pleasure of her leading a reflective tour of an exhibition at the Walker Art Gallery[2] in Liverpool on behalf of Art and Christianity.[3] It is no surprise that her perspective on kindness is creative and effusive:

> A conversation about kindness is exactly the kind of nourishing, holistic experience that I love to have. I connect kindness with imagination itself. In the gift of imagination, one of our God-given opportunities in the life that we have is to attempt and fail and attempt and fail to live life well. Kindness is imaginative creativity in response to relationships, communities and God's work in every life. Kindness is not always my default realm, but I wish it were – it's a light I want to travel by. In its light, which is a radiant response to God's invitation, God's expectation, God's gift, we might see more clearly how to love courageously and seek justice honestly even when it's costly. It's no small thing to pause, breathe and consider in any moment, 'Is this kind?' and then to act accordingly. The answer might be 'no', and then, personally, I try to return to the gift of imagination and what Joan Chittister describes as 'the monastery of the heart'. I find kindness there and follow it as best I can. When I think about kindness, I think about that line from the Eucharist: all things come from you, and of your own do we give you.

> It all belongs to God. Kindness flows from the heart of God. God is a pure being, and kindness is a name for God. It's not just 'God is kind', it's that 'kindness is God'. Kindness is a 'fruit of the Spirit' in Paul's letter to the Galatians (5.22). Kindness is a divine name.

There is so much beauty in what Ayla is proclaiming here – God is all in all and all that is, is God. Ayla refers to Janet Soskice's excellent book *The Kindness of God: Metaphor, gender, and religious language*,[4] where the author is concerned to challenge the feminizing language of kindness by deconstructing patriarchal notions of the loving-kindness of God. Ayla explains: 'There's an unhelpful, misogynistic feminization of the notion of kindness where, because of perhaps its wider association with tenderness, with a particular kind of care, it's easily forgotten by us that kindness is a fruit of the Spirit.'[5]

These are fruits that flourish in a healthy faith. An institution that is not fruitful in the spiritual sense is not health-giving and its members will not flourish. Seeking kindness, praying for these fruits to be manifest, is the work of the Church not just the individual. It is in the seeking of these fruits, Ayla argues, that justice will emerge as a work of prayer in the light of kindness:

> The relationship between justice and kindness is really close. It's active and alive. I think that the desire to be kind, like the desire for beauty and art, is a yearning for justice for all living things, especially in relation to oppression and a longing for the world to be a better place. To deeply long for 'the peace which the world cannot give',[6] or will not give, is, I think, an act of kindness in itself. It's an orientation towards goodness that depends on God's own peace abiding in us, if we would only recognize it. Regarding kindness and prayer, the longer I am a Christian and a priest, the more mysterious prayer becomes. It is as steadfast as it is elusive (and kindness can be like that too). I don't really think any of us can ever know fully about the relationship between the prayers of the people and our kind-hearted God, but I trust that praying itself is an act of kindness.

Ayla points out that this deep prayerful longing for kindness articulated here is most evident in the Eucharist. Ayla insists that 'the sacraments are kind. What is kinder than the sacrificial love of the crucifixion transforming into the eternal holiness of the resurrection promised to each of us? Jesus' life, and death, and life again, was, is and will be radically kind.'

36

Mercy not sacrifice

Steven Shakespeare, professor of philosophy

13 October 2025

May the divine Liberator
drive us far from dreams of domination.
May the divine Weaver
make us new hearts of compassion.
May the divine Healer
teach us to cherish our shared family.
Amen.

Steven Shakespeare[1]

Steven Shakespeare is Professor of Philosophy at Liverpool Hope University;[2] he's a writer of fiction, philosophy, poetry and prayers. Steven explains that his 'writing emerges from my intellectual, pastoral and spiritual interests'. I ask him how he views kindness; he responds by reasoning that there is a 'a vulnerability and strength in kindness, which is about being attentive to someone and being present to somebody in an authentic way. Just being with someone for the sake of it and acknowledging their humanity.'

Steven explains that for him kindness 'interrupts the drive towards productivity', something that is evident in his work – particularly his poems and prayers. They are written for mercy's sake, not driven as output. 'Trying to hold open a space of encounter so that something else can happen between people,' he says.

> The priority to me is what's incarnated; there are those moments in the scriptural witness where that kind of incarnate kindness comes, for instance in the Benedictus. It's translated in the Anglican office as 'the

> tender compassion of our God', and the Catholic office translates it as 'the loving-kindness of the heart of our God', which I really love.
>
> I think in encountering that reality of another person, you're always encountering an icon of God. And there's something of God in that relationship. If we think of God as Trinity, the heart of that is that shared kindness, and relationality and making space for the other.

Steven is proposing that at the heart of the impulse for kindness is the desire for human connection, and in relation to God a spiritual connection. Our Christian trinitarian God is the epitome of relational kindness. Human kindness then can be seen as a response to this glorious kindness huddle as we long for interconnected relationships that honour our uniqueness. 'So, if kindness is a kind of attentiveness to the person, it also must be a respect for their dignity, mystery, irreplaceability. So, justice is about what is due to people to allow them to flourish in that. God desires mercy not sacrifice.'

I wonder how his work, Hope University and our ecumenical ambitions might foster kindness to seek the common good. Steven contends that this requires asking some fundamental questions about institutional priorities:

> It shouldn't be that kindness is a kind of little star in the darkness of this cold, indifferent world, but that somehow it irradiates it, and our politics, our structures, our businesses in some way need to be asking that question. How are we going about our business, universities, churches in a way that is kind? For the people who work here, the people we interact with, to the earth – is what we are doing going to provoke loving-kindness? Is this going to foster that kind of relationality and presence and attention? Or is it not? Is it going to destroy it?

Those of us who work in anchor institutions such as universities, churches, hospitals, schools etc., should be able to ask these fundamental kindness questions. And those social and cultural institutions that prioritize people above production and output, who are brave and self-assured, should be robust enough to respond with clarity and vision.

37

Fiercely kind

Hannah Rich, Director, Christians on the Left

15 October 2025

God,
Keep my anger from becoming meanness.
Keep my sorrow from collapsing into self-pity.
Keep my heart soft enough to keep breaking.
Keep my anger turned towards justice, not cruelty.
Remind me that all of this, every bit of it, is for love.
Keep me fiercely kind.
Amen.

Laura Jean Truman[1]

Hannah Rich is Director of Christians on the Left[2] and a researcher at Theos Think Tank.[3] Hannah is used to speaking truth to power, she also knows what it is like to be exhausted by activism. She has come to our conversation with a prayer written by Laura Jean Truman[4] (the last few lines are quoted above) and as she reads it the words touch my poor exhausted heart. This is how Hannah and I are feeling today, and we need this 'Prayer for the Tired Angry Ones'. The idea that we can be *fiercely kind* is such a relief to hear. It is very easy to let our desire for justice become hard or brittle and our language mean.

One of the ways I recently knew I was burning out was because I started to be less kind in my direct approaches to people when challenging injustice. This prayer came at the right time for me. Hannah explains why this prayer has spoken to her:

> Justice feels relentless, the need to do justice feels relentless, but in that, the one thing we're called to be is fiercely kind. And I love that, because

> that encapsulates everything I'd ever hope to be and hope to demonstrate in my work. In fact, I'd want on my gravestone, 'Hannah is fiercely kind'. Kindness isn't rolling over, isn't just being nice. Fiercely kind feels like what the world needs, so people who are passionate about stuff, who care about justice, who care about a better world, and are able to do that with compassion, and with love, and with kindness, but without that taking the edge off the urgency and the passion, the fierceness, with which they feel stuff.

The first time I met Hannah I knew she was a kind person, a *fiercely kind* person, and she spoke with such clarity and humility about justice issues. She was leading a research project commissioned by Theos and Church Urban Fund called GRA:CE.[5] This project explored the relationship between social action, discipleship and church growth. Hannah led this research with a sure-sighted diligence that gave the project credibility. The same can be said about her work with MPs: Hannah speaks into their work with a determined kindness. She points out, as Andy Flannagan (a former Director of Christians on the Left) also noted, that the public can easily be misled by the media into dehumanizing MPs or placing them on pedestals:

> Many people said, 'Oh, I wish we had more MPs that were like Jo Cox', or 'Wouldn't it be lovely if everyone was as nice as this David Amess guy seems to have been?' 'Isn't it a shame that we're only learning that now he's been murdered?' But most of the MPs I encounter, most of the people in senior places in public life that I'm lucky enough to get to work with are that. They are kind people.

I am sure Hannah is right; there are many fiercely kind people in public office. The challenge is that the systems these people create and then maintain don't always appear to be built on kind principles:

> If our economic system and our political system was based on people, then it would inherently be a bit kinder, even if kindness wasn't framed as the driving factor in that; if we had an economy that works for people, rather than for the system it would just be kinder by default.
>
> It's the same as our politics. I'm really lucky that I get to see the humans within the political system, and yet somehow a system that is just a sum of loads of humans still isn't itself human, or humanized.

The theme of dehumanized systems is emerging time and time again in these kindness conversations. Whether in church, economics, politics, academia and other key anchor organizations, the systems that have been designed for life are sucking the life and kindness from us. As Eve Poole has pointed out, this doesn't bode well for the future that will be designed by robots – if the humans can't create humanizing systems, how will the robots be able to do a better job?

The bedrock of Hannah's kindness is her Christian faith; this is what calls her to engage in issues of social justice:

> My faith is what gives me that fierceness to want to change the world, naive as that might sound, and that kind of drive to change things. That must be underpinned by a kindness, because that was the way Jesus did things. He came to serve and not be served, and there's a model of humility and of kindness and of gentleness. Jesus was all those things, but he was also a revolutionary, and a radical, and he politically shook things up and did things that people didn't like. I think that he probably did them kindly – he's not just judging but he gets to the heart of the matter. The story of the woman by the well, where he talks to her about how many husbands she's had, he was really kind ... you can imagine the tone of the voice with which that was said. He was really kind, and yet fierce in terms of, 'I see you. I see all that you are, and I'm going to love that, but I'm also going to challenge.' That as a model for faith is valuable. If you look at who Jesus was, he was unswervingly kind.

38

Bees

David Primrose, beekeeper and former cathedral canon

15 October 2025

> Honeybees are our inspiration because they pollinate the world with their kindness, helping fertilize plants, flowers, trees, and making honey. Without honeybees, our world would be a dark place. We, like bees, need to pollinate the world with kindness to make sure our world is full of light.
>
> *The Honey Foundation, Arizona*[1]

David Primrose is an apiarist – a beekeeper; he is a retired Church of England priest, formerly a canon at Lichfield Cathedral and lead for social responsibility in the Diocese of Lichfield. David is a great mentor and spiritual director to me; he is one of the kindest people I know. David is aware of his kindness; indeed, David's self-awareness is what makes him an excellent spiritual director – David knows himself very well. And as such he can look into the soul of another and confidently ask questions without creating anxiety or suffering.

> I am fairly intensely pro-social and desire other people to be included and not to be left behind. Also, I've got a fair level of both self-awareness and awareness of others around. So those two things together mean that other people have noticed that I have adjusted my behaviour for their well-being, and therefore other people have told me I'm kind, so I have come to accept that, as it's a common enough label that comes my way that it's true by other people's validation rather than my own perception of myself.

David describes kindness in social terms: 'Kind people make sure that the whole collective carries on together, because they're the people who make the necessary adjustments for the people who might otherwise get injured, or hurt, or left behind in the process.' There is a robust self-assured clarity to the way David speaks of kindness. It is both natural and a practice for him. He sets time aside for kindness and cultivates it in himself and others.

> I feel sufficiently robust in myself that I can afford to absorb a reasonable amount of stress, or other people's distress, without feeling that I need to push back to maintain my own stability or integrity. I've got the capacity to absorb quite a lot of other people's angst, or even negativity; if they choose to focus negativity upon myself and they don't get a pushback response, then it does dissipate.

This is an aspect of kindness that I haven't explored with any other contributor: the development of self-awareness and containment that allows for kindness to be less costly and more effective. One of my observations has been that those people who are able to accept their kindness appear to be more able to freely offer kindness without counting the cost; they appear to have pockets full of kindness to spare. It is as if confidence and experience allows people to be less guarded and fearful of running out of kindness. It is important for David that he not only has the capacity to offer kindness to others but that he is also able to ensure his own safety and ability to maintain kindness to himself. He explains that as kindness is a value he cherishes it is entwined in his own sense of self: 'I've got the capacity to absorb quite a lot of hostility before I feel who I am is being jeopardized by this.'

It is David's self-awareness and fierce determination to maintain his values, particularly the value of kindness, that make him such a treasured spiritual director and colleague. I am grateful for his confidence and insightful wisdom.

39

Cultivating kindness

Chine McDonald, writer and Director of Theos

16 October 2025

> You have given gifts,
> But you have not given gifts of love,
> You have not given with a kindly heart.
> You would already have been robbed of your life,
> If I had known earlier of the danger.
>
> *Marcel Mauss, Hreidmar, a hero of the Edda saga, replies to the curse of Loki*[1]

Chine McDonald describes herself as a 'mother of two young boys, they're seven and three, I'm a wife of Mark, a Yorkshireman. We live in south-east London. I'm Director of Theos, which is a Christian think tank based in Westminster. I'm also a trustee of my church, and Greenbelt and Christian Aid.' So it is safe to say Chine is a busy person! And it is this busyness that becomes the focus of our conversation as I am interested in how she manages to maintain kindness in the hubbub of her hectic life:

> One of the reasons why I'm so busy is because I find it very difficult to say no. I am a people pleaser in my DNA, and I really like making people happy, sometimes to my detriment. So I think in people's interactions with me they might see me doing something that's acting against my own self-interest or just trying to make sure that everyone's OK. I like harmony, balance, I feel everyone's emotions if I walk into a room – which can be a burden sometimes, and I'm kind of oversensitive. I'm a worrier. There is something in me that wants to make people happy, and I feel like there are easy ways of doing that. Kind words, kind acts ... So that's kind of my constant to-do list, it's the work, but it's also, 'Is everyone I know OK?' I think I find unkindness ... awful.

What is apparent is that kindness is a priority for Chine. It is both basic and fundamental. Kindness is also something Chine has given a great deal of thought to:

> Kindness is about both the act of doing something kind and also receiving kindness. It's always kind of two-sided. It is one of the things that I explored in my theology degree; my sociology of religion part of it was this idea of gift exchange in societies and communities and tribes over history. There's a lot of discussion about whether you can ever give a free gift to someone. So thinkers like Marcel Mauss[2] and Bronisław Malinowski[3] discussed this idea and I've always found it fascinating. I love being kind, I love doing kind things for people ... so is it actually a selfish thing?

The idea that any gift, whether it be an object or a kindness, is ever truly given without a sense of reciprocity has been a concern of many contributors to this project. But for many others this has been an affirmation of their sense that kindness is a communal act where all involved are blessed. The idea that everyone involved in any sort of kindness is included in the positive exchange is something that many of us feel is a vital part of what makes kindness so impactful. Its effect is amplified when noticed, acknowledged and shared. Kindness is in 'solidarity with human need'.[4]

I ask Chine how she thinks we the people of God in our churches enhance kindness and seek the common good. She insists this is happening, but that we don't prioritize kindness stories:

> The Church is doing so much in its local communities – feeding people who haven't got food, giving shelter to people who haven't got homes, helping people out of debt. The number of volunteer hours that go into helping people around us as churches is stunning. Unfortunately, I just don't think people associate the Church with kindness. We did some polling at Theos a few weeks ago which found that at least half of people don't know anything about what good the Church does in society. People don't know that the Church helps homeless people, and helps people out of debt, etc. So, it's not just about doing the kind things ... How can we be so good at doing kind things that we're known for being kind? Maybe sometimes the stories of abuse, or the stories of divide and power and debate shout louder in the newspapers than the smaller acts. So, if we can sort out negatives, the big stories, then we can be known for being a people of kindness.

40

Our God is a great big God

Year Five, St Cleopas C of E Primary School[1]

17 October 2025

> They stood still, looking sad. Then one of them, whose name was Cleopas, answered him, 'Are you the only stranger in Jerusalem who does not know the things that have taken place there in these days?' He asked them, 'What things?' They replied, 'The things about Jesus of Nazareth ...'
>
> *Cleopas unknowingly speaking to Jesus on the Road to Emmaus, Luke 24.13–32*

I have the pleasure of being invited to speak about kindness to Year Five at one of my wonderful local schools. It's lunch break when I arrive – I'm greeted at the gate by a large group of small children all dressed in red. They tell me that it is 'Show Racism the Red Card' day,[2] so they are allowed to wear red to school. As an Everton fan this seems to me to be a bit unfair. When I raise this with Year Five, they tell me that there are only a few of my kind at St Cleopas and they 'just have to cope for the day'. I must admit my kindness vibes are a bit conflicted at this response. But faced with a room full of Liverpool fans all bedecked in replica football kits I give it my best shot.

To my surprise, when I ask what colour kindness might be, none of them say red. Nearly all of them say green because 'it's correct', and it's the 'colour of the grass'. That said, one of the children does go for blue because 'it's the colour of Mary'. They all agree that not everyone is naturally kind – but all think *they* are kind. They also agree that God is '100 per cent kind'. They tell me that one of the kindest people they know is George – although this appears to come as a surprise to George! He takes the compliment well. They also list their mums and their teacher among their kindest people. Mo Salah also gets a kindness mention, as do various pets.

I am loving their enthusiasm and imagination about what kindness means to them. By this time a couple of the children are getting fidgety. I think lunch is kicking in and it seems like a good idea to ask them if they know about kindness songs. At this point they get up and spontaneously start to sing 'Our God is a great big God' with the appropriate actions. I get sucked into the pure joy and hilarity of the moment.

I wonder where they think kindness comes from and they tell me that it comes from your heart, from God, from the soul, and it's just natural. Their optimism and willingness to share moves me, particularly as they start to tell some stories of kindness. Here are some of their experiences:

> My brother choked on a chip, but it came out and he was OK. Then my brother and dad prayed together.
>
> At a sleepover with my best friend, I fell off a chair and they helped me back up.
>
> I gave my leftover food to a homeless man.
>
> My brother's clothes became too small for him, so he gave them to me.
>
> My dad bought a homeless man a Big Mac.
>
> My auntie adopted a dog that was being harmed.

When I ask them about what would make the world a kinder place, they tell me:

> Compliments
> Not littering
> Stopping war
> If everyone was kind
> Stopping racism
> Being respectful to everyone
> Everyone loving each other.

From the mouths of Year Five children, this wisdom seems so easy and hopeful. I know their lives are not always stress-free. Living in the inner city isn't straightforward. But these children on this day are kind – to me and to each other.

Even though they are all Liverpool fans.

41

Soft power

Rosemarie Mallett, Bishop of Croydon

22 October 2025

> The LORD is my light and my salvation;
> whom shall I fear?
> The LORD is the stronghold of my life;
> of whom shall I be afraid?
>
> *Psalm 27.1*

Rosemarie Mallett and I meet online at 11 a.m. on a soggy morning in October. Rosemarie is in her office drinking her third coffee having already had three meetings that morning. I am grateful for the hour we have together talking about kindness. We were due to meet yesterday, but she had been delayed in a consultation with diocesan clergy colleagues about the rise of nationalism and the impact this was having on their work for unity and diversity. This was a good meeting where she felt people could 'Give their testimonies, and speak to their reality, whether they all usually met together or not ... the room felt safe enough.' Creating space for people to speak their truth is important to Rosemarie. Throughout our time together she shares examples of how community, collaboration and care foster kindness.

For Rosemarie kindness is:

> Compassion and care. Which may sound the same, but compassion is something that is of a heart, that we feel. And care is something that we can offer. It's an inflection within. And then it's an outward manifestation for us, for me, as a Christian, of living with the grace of God, recognizing that we stand under that grace, which is compassionate and loving and ... therefore, we receive that kindness, and then we're asked to offer it to others, because it's as we receive, so we should give.

> So that's what the two words together mean when I hear the word kindness.

Rosemarie is committed to community engagement – something she has cultivated throughout her ministry. While many bishops lose this grass-roots connection, Rosemarie has maintained it and sees this as vital to the way she practises kindness and her ministry. She describes South London Listens, a Citizens UK-led health taskforce that she is a co-chair of, that has been meeting for over four years. This group has, in Rosemarie's words,

> been enabling the community to be co-creators of the change that they want to see with regard to health and well-being, and in particular around mental health and well-being. And it grew as a movement post-Covid, when we recognized that particularly young people in our communities were going to struggle with mental well-being. But then we also realized that our refugee communities were going to struggle, our asylum-seeker communities were going to struggle, our diverse communities from the backgrounds that people saw that were going to struggle, Latin American communities were going to struggle. And so, what has come together is the partnership work with Citizens, three major south London Health Boards and local citizens. I sit as co-convenor with the three executive chairs of the health boards, and I am just the bishop, with these three executive chairs. They've got thousands of people that they are responsible for, staff and patients, and the power to make decisions that will change people's health options and their lives.
>
> I sit on this board, and I go, so why am I here? You know, because I'm the only person in the room on that panel that can't make people make change happen. But they say to me 'Bishop Rosemarie, your presence is needed, this is our ask. Will you continue to work for justice for us? Will you continue to be loving, caring and compassionate towards us and the people we serve, and will you model that as a leader?'
>
> That's the only power that I hold … my soft power.[1]

It strikes me that what Rosemarie has identified here is a crucial aspect of kindness, that, once triggered in the context of community and in pursuit of justice, becomes a powerful tool for social change. It might seem soft – in the sense of it being without levers – but its reach is extensive, and its impact is powerful. By extending loving-kindness in this way Rosemarie relinquishes control of power and releases it to those who can activate change, whether that be to the chairs of the health boards or the community who are also becoming the receivers of the change that is being activated. This exciting, fluid and dynamic exchange of power is what makes real lasting social change happen.

Rosemarie was influenced by her experience of working with the Maryknoll Sisters in Tanzania:[2]

> The heart of what they did was serve God at base level with communities, offering their gifts and their skills, to enable others to have agency, and I could see that, in terms of the work that they did. I met these women of God, from the Maryknolls, who were activists, who were engaged in making a difference to the societies in which they lived. I just found them totally, totally inspirational in terms of how to put faith into action.

Rosemarie cites Psalm 27 as the Bible passage that:

> just absolutely gave me the capacity in times of trial to hold on and just keep going, and to believe a bit more in myself, and to believe that God had a purpose for me ... beyond the despair ... that God had gifted me in a particular way, and he had gifted me that way because he had a reason and purpose for my life.

Similarly, she says the Magnificat is 'a heart song, if you believe in justice, social justice. A woman singing ... singing for justice. A woman who was going to bear the light of the world in her womb.'

When I ask Rosemarie who inspires her to kindness, she commends her diocesan bishop, the Bishop of Southwark, Christopher Chessun. She describes him as 'someone who makes time for everyone. Someone who tries to remember the names of all those he meets and truly prays for them.' I was impressed by the kindness of this collegiality and her willingness to openly express her appreciation. It was a tender moment. Another example of the soft power of kindness.

42

No wrath in God

June Raymond, Sister, Notre Dame de Namur

25 October 2025

> [Julian of Norwich's] unselfconscious use of feminine, maternal imagery about God comes to us as a promise of the inclusiveness of God's nature; her message of the steadfast, unalterable, unjudging love of God reaches out to those who have felt excluded by organised religion; her profound hopefulness reaches out to a world in turmoil, offering us the dream of the merciful tide of God's power that cannot be diverted by human nature.
>
> *Jane Williams*[1]

June Raymond is a Notre Dame de Namur Sister,[2] who lives in community near Southport. It is in the small cosy living room at the convent that we meet, as we have done many times. Sr June has been my spiritual mentor for nearly 30 years. Sr June (aka 'the healing nun') has worked powerful acts of healing for many people over the years, and it is this ministry that marks her out as a kind person.

Sr June explains:

> Kindness in my work is being able to be intelligently alongside a person that I am understanding. I'm in tune with who they really are and what's really going on for them. One of my early clients was somebody who came in not able to walk and I did some work with her and some stuff that really needed doing. Next time she came and she was walking by herself – and at some point, she said, 'the most important thing you did for me, you heard me', and I kept that as being the most important thing I do.

My experience of working spiritually with Sr June is that she hears me at a level beyond speaking. When we pray together I feel she isn't just hearing my words, but she is also hearing my soul. She explains that this praying is partly intuitive but it is also a learned gift:

> I learned that prayer is not just something in your head, it's using the awareness of your whole body to be in tune with the whole of the variety of emotions and with the natural world as well, and from there going to doing healing. And when I was doing healing, I would tune in with all that wellness and so the more I did it the more I developed that sense until I could slip into it quite easily.

Sr June works healing using Bach Flower Remedies. She explains that the remedies help to reveal 'the negative in you as the positive waiting to happen' and enables the person struggling to 'look at the shadow and have it transformed as a gift'. I can testify to this truth. Time after time I have come to Sr June with knotty problems, physical pain, trauma and deep sadness. Time and time again we have sat and prayed ... and she has sent me away with a tiny bottle of flower remedy-laced brandy ... and I have seen transformation. Deep healing has happened.

Today, I express my gratitude for the spiritual guidance she has offered and how this has sustained me over many years. I am grateful for her ministry. Sr June tells me that her cancer has returned and that there is nothing more the doctors can do. Perhaps she can have some radiotherapy to ease the symptoms, but she is at peace with this. 'All shall be well, and all shall be well, and all manner of things shall be well.' She quotes Julian of Norwich as she repeats the prayer she says every day:

> God of your goodness give yourself to me, for thou art enough for me and if I ask for anything less I shall never be satisfied. Only in thee I have all.[3]

Sr June and I sit quietly for a while.

I am taking in her news. And shamefully I am thinking of myself as much as I am worried for her. I don't want my sister to be sick and die. I can't bear another loss. I want her to be healed. Healer, heal yourself.

The silence is broken by a story about the kindest woman Sr June knows. June explains that this person is a recovering alcoholic with a 'lot of courage in her suffering', who works with the 'most damaged people you could ever meet'. When Sr June asked, 'What is your greatest asset?' the woman thought about it and replied that it is all that she hates most in herself because that is what gives her the ability to be alongside the most damaged and to say to them, 'I have been there and done that.' Sr June explains, 'That woman is full of empathy and that is what makes her kind.'

We sit again in silence.

Since Sr June moved back to the community house, I have brought my dog, Tig, to visit. He loves playing in the garden and visiting sisters in their rooms. He lets himself in through open doors and they seem fine with this. Sr June and I agree that when my husband died, and then shortly afterwards my first dog Jacob, I was grieving so deeply that Tig saved my life. Sr June reminds me that there is goodness even in sorrow and that only God and our dogs know what faithfulness is. Then Sr June recites Carmen Bernos de Gasztold, 'The Prayer of the Dog'.[4]

We laugh and I give her a hug. We don't usually hug. It is time to leave the quiet and return to the city.

As I leave, Sr June insists, 'God is kind, there is no wrath in God.'

43

A work in progress

Michael Leyden, Dean, Emmanuel Theological College

27 October 2025

> As we walk the way with Jesus, then, we are relearning the human vocation, called to live and work with God for our good and the good of all creation.
>
> *Jane Williams*[1]

Michael Leyden is Dean of Emmanuel Theological College;[2] he is a priest, writer and theologian with a particular interest in ethics and leadership. As we begin, Michael tells me that he is writing a book about Christian character and has been reading about kindness as part of his research. During his research, Michael has noticed:

> In wider discourses around leadership and psychology of leadership, there are a lot of people outside of the church saying, 'We're not very good at kindness and humanity in leadership.' So they're looking to the Church for help and, weirdly, we've spent quite a lot of time looking outside of the Church to figure out what leadership is about.

I wonder if the Church seeking a worldly way of managing, organizing, creating structures etc. has led us to forget our *raison d'être* – that we are led by spiritual ethics and gifts. What makes us unique and attractive should go ahead of all our systems and structures, and presence ahead of growth. With this resonating in my head, I ask Michael what he thinks kindness is, and he replies:

> I think the first thing for me is that kindness is about recognizing someone's innate worth and dignity as a human. I think Christians should be better at it. Not necessarily than other people, but just better at it

> than we are, and one of the reasons for that is it's a fruit of the Spirit. If you're growing close to God, if your roots are going down deep into the life of the Spirit as a Christian disciple, you just expect to be more loving, more joyful, more peaceful, more patient, more kind. Because there's something in us, that we're supposed to become more like Jesus. So, if the spirit is at work in our lives, forget the power stuff; if you meet nasty Christians, unkind Christians, you've got to wonder, how deep do your roots go?

Michael notes that the 'more anxious and fearful we become, the less kind to one another we are'. He asserts that the Church of England is going through a particularly difficult, anxious phase, and 'there's something about fear, fear about survival'. This is creating a lack of confidence in ministry, which is in danger of leading to a lack of compassion that 'voids kindness in us'. One of the ways Michael hopes Emmanuel College can respond to this is by engaging in conversations with students about virtue ethics.[3] Fostering good conversation about ethics and morality. 'Kindness is one of those absolute gems of a virtue theory, that takes investment. The more you practise it, the more natural it will be.'

I am excited about Emmauel College focusing on kindness as a primary virtue for leadership – being inspired to seek the fruits[4] and guided by the gifts of the Spirit.[5] Michael acknowledges that this approach takes time and requires significant investment from the individual and the systems that enable them to flourish. A whole system needs to be in place to support students not just in formation but in developing sustainable long-term ministries. In this sense, kindness is countercultural as it requires time, and, as Michael puts it, 'time is costly. The pace at which we live inhibits kindness – it inhibits us having the time to see people, and to attend to people, and to respond to people.' Michael has a vision for leadership that values kindness:

> If kindness is about people, then actually it flies in the face of the language of achievement and success because it's about saying, who's this person in front of me? Where are they? What's their story? What's their name? What does it mean to give them time and attention? And to see them.

Taking time for kindness is a reoccurring theme in these conversations. The value of kindness, and the cost of ignoring this value, feels like an investment the Church and other anchor institutions should be making as a matter of urgency.

44

Million-pound miracle mortgage

Gill Morgan, retired tax inspector

27 October 2025

> Don't become so well-adjusted to your culture that you fit into it without even thinking. Instead, fix your attention on God. You'll be changed from the inside out.
>
> *Romans 12.2 (*The Message*)*

Gill Morgan is a retired 'ground-breaking tax inspector, becoming one of the most senior women at the Inland Revenue'.[1] She lives in Surrey with her husband Ken. In their expansive garden they have created Narnia, which is entered through a wardrobe in the woods. There is a massive tree house that towers above the front garden, a swimming pool that is almost constantly in use during the summer, a clearing where hot chocolate and marshmallows are served, and a small steam train that you can sit on encircles the camp. The Dell (the name of their house)[2] is a magical place of welcome and joy. I have been playing there for 45 years. During that time, Gill and Ken have often helped me to keep my faith together and keep my eyes on Jesus. Once you are in their lives you are their children and you are welcome any time. As Gill explains, 'Not knowingly have I ever ruled anybody out of my life.'

Gill is 82 and she and Ken have been living with the open house policy all their married life. 'It always takes me by surprise,' Gill tells me, '... particularly when you get to my age, I'm staggered people still want to come. I am surprised. I often think, golly, a pair of old fogies like us, what ... what is going on? It's wonderful. Totally wonderful.'

I remind Gill that they have a steam train in their garden and a swimming pool – who wouldn't want to visit! Though for me it's not the promise of meeting Mr Tumnus that draws me to their home, it's their company – their solid, reassuring, steady and, most importantly, kind welcome. And they have never judged. They have reprimanded me but never judged.

I want to tell you a story, it is my testimony to the Lord's grace and loving-kindness; God cast Gill and Ken as angels. When I was in my late twenties, for various very complicated reasons, I managed to accrue a large personal debt – student loans, bad investments, overspending, and I took on my Mark's bad debts. I owed the banks, friends, credit cards etc. I was very frightened and ashamed and had no idea where to turn. In the past I had asked my dad to bail me out, but this was big. I had also been running away from God for a while and had thought I had shaken my evangelical past off in the haze of pop music and boys. I had attempted to declare myself an atheist and, although I was still praying, I felt sure I didn't believe in the God I was talking to. Then one day I didn't have any more money. I had a good job as a lecturer at a university, a car, I was married and had a baby ... but I had absolutely no more money. I panicked and turned to the only people I knew who had any idea about finance: Gill and Ken – a tax inspector and an accountant. So I rolled up at their door and asked for help, and they welcomed me and scolded me gently and then offered me advice. Rather than suggesting a parental bail-out or a loan, Ken advised bankruptcy. A *big*, absolute and serious option – but I needed a serious option. Ken was clear that I needed to face this and start again. To ask forgiveness from the law and draw a line under it. We prayed, he explained the process and I booked a day in court. I faced the judge, then the official receiver, and my financial affairs fell into the hands of the law. I had nothing. It was devastating.

One Sunday shortly after my court appearance, I went to church for the first time in years and they welcomed me. It was a break from my self-hatred for an hour, a rest for my weary soul. The next week I went again. Then a few weeks later I was sitting in a straight-backed pew looking at the stained-glass window above the high altar and I felt this overwhelming call on my life. I didn't hear God's voice, but I felt an obligation to an absurd idea – that I should let myself be forgiven and be a priest. I burst into tears and sobbed. Why would God want me to be a priest when I couldn't even manage to be a solvent lecturer. How would that happen? But it did. It took a while, because rather sensibly the Bishop knew I needed to be discharged from bankruptcy, which took two years, then he wanted me to wait another five years. I was ordained in 2008.

Gill and Ken were there through all that; they were there when my mum (who lived nearby) was ill, and when she died I stayed at their house. Gill calls me most weeks and challenges and encourages me; she suggests books for me to read, sends cards and WhatsApp messages. Gill hasn't ever accepted a mediocre response from me, particularly if it is about my faith or family. Kindness is complicated and can be uncomfortable, but it always wants the best, always demands the best. I have learned a lot about kindness from Gill and Ken, and for that I shall always be grateful.

During our conversation Gill tells me that they have bought the land next door to their house. Gill explains the vision:

> It's all a miracle. We have a million-pound mortgage because we want to live well now. Having assets doesn't help anybody. So, we've bought the next place down the bridleway – Webb's riding stables. It's got 12 stables, and a bungalow with 5 bedrooms. It will need a bit of work. But the exciting thing, Ellen, is I did a bit of research, and in Wokingham there is a fabulous charity we're going to visit. They offer equine therapy for teenagers, for young people. Their mission statement is 'to walk alongside young people and families, showing love and acceptance according to Christian principles, encouraging brave and positive choices'. So, that's what we are doing next in our life of a long obedience in the same direction.[3]

45

Little fires

Azariah France-Williams, priest, writer and broadcaster

28 October 2025

> Until our institutions are reordered, our education systems, our political systems, and our church systems, a person of colour does not have the societal backing and reinforcement to flourish.
>
> *Azariah France-Williams*[1]

Azariah France-Williams is Rector of Ascension Church, Hulme, Manchester; he is a writer and broadcaster. Azariah has a vision for a red-hot uprising of love and kindness. Hearing it inspired me:

> I don't know what society needs. But I want to start with my influences. I remember hearing an African-American preacher that said over and over again, as you influence the world you're in, God will increase your world of influence. So, how can I foster a culture where we can meet one another, across difference, across class, across race, and discover our common humanity, and celebrate our differences, not hide from them. I've got the spaces where I have influence – I think a number of us have – and we can create lots of little fires, which then can come together and create a real furnace of love and kindness.

This idea of lighting small beacon fires of kindness at the hyper-local level that then inspire a furnace of love and kindness is infectious. Azariah made me think we could all do this. Together we could make a seismic kindness shift if we determinedly commit to it within our spheres of influence. After all, this is how massive change begins, at a local level, until enough leverage is built up for the architecture of a system to be redesigned. So

I ask Azariah what he thinks might be the practical requirements for kindness?

> During the pandemic, there were a number of people who discovered the names of their neighbours. People began to value those that are at the bottom of the ladder in terms of recognition and status in society – our key workers. Although it made us face our mortality, it restored something of our humanity as well. It was like a temporary moment where we recognized that we were more of a community. That extended globally as well, in terms of the scientists working together. People began to think, 'OK, there may be another way of doing this and living this life.'
>
> Those sorts of pressured scenarios, that kind of breaking gives the opportunity for some kind of humanity to peek out. But then it's too easy to go back to default settings, to factory settings. The spell has worn off now, the honeymoon period is well and truly over. But it feels like there are these moments where a deeper, more communal version of humanity rises to the surface before it sinks back or is dragged back by commercialism and capitalism and colonialism ... ways in which, the few take charge of and take the benefits of the many.

Azariah's observations about the rise of kindness during the pandemic have been noted by others I have spoken to. As has been the disappointment of the post-pandemic resetting of the more selfish default. How quickly we seemed to accept that the bright colours of Oz were just a temporary hope, and how quickly we let the world return to the monochrome of Kansas. The fires of kindness went out and the coals of love went cold. But perhaps we are waking up again? Perhaps the people of God are stoking the grate and are ready for a new wave of kindness? Azariah believes that this is possible if we act from our resources and not overreach our capacity. He explains: 'It's recognizing there is value in doing what you can, not what you can't.' I agree that working in solidarity, sharing resources, being aware of our limitations and allowing others to burn alongside us is a practical way of kindness. 'Just love what is in front of us.'

Azariah told this story about doing what is possible, working from your gifts and giving what you can to the cause of kindness:

> We used to live near where the Grenfell fire happened, and my wife Anna and I went for a couple of days just to help with the relief effort. We went the day after it caught fire, and it was still smouldering when

we got there. There was a number of people who had come out of the apartment block and they were sat dejected at the side of the road, just huddled together, thousand-yard stare. But then behind them was a young man playing the violin, just playing the most beautiful classical music. You could still see the smoke, you could see the smouldering of the flats behind him. It was a really beautiful moment.

Later I bumped into him, and I said, 'Why did you do that?' He said, 'When I saw it on the news and I thought I can't organize some big relief effort or whatever, but I can play the violin. So I thought I'd just come and play the violin.'

There's such beauty and such worth in the offering of that gift. This is all any of us can do, offer the little fire of kindness and hope it grows into a positive furnace of something that can change the world for the better.

46

God is kind

Stephen Cottrell, Archbishop of York

29 October 2025

Ask yourself what you really want for Christmas.

Is it not this peace? Is it not this good will? Is it not this hope?

See it, seek it and savour it in the very best that you can be, and in the best of what you see around you in courageous leadership that seeks peace, and in all the tiny acts of kindness that oil the wheels of goodness.

Stephen Cottrell[1]

Stephen Cottrell has just got back from Rome where he joined King Charles III to meet Pope Leo XIV at the Vatican. During their time together a British monarch and a Pope prayed in the Sistine Chapel for the first time since the Reformation. Stephen referred to the experience as humbling and an important moment in history. It was an ecumenical joy to see both Catholic and Anglican English Archbishops together in this Catholic Jubilee Year.[2] This was a very public kindness – a demonstration of affection and respect. A rare opportunity to show a kinship and a solidarity. So, this is where we start our kindness conversation:

I think I understand kindness to be that generous, tender-hearted reaching out, one to another. And although I'm not a great linguist, I've always understood that the root of the old English word 'kind', or the word 'kindness', is another English word kin, i.e., those who are members of our family, or indeed our extended family. From a Christian point of view I find this a helpful way into thinking what kindness means. It means to treat everybody as your sister and your brother. To recognize the responsibilities we have, one to another.

Kindness as a Christian virtue is right at the very heart of what it means to live in that acknowledgement that we belong to one another, that we have responsibilities to one another, and that we need to reach out to one another. It's those large and little acts of tenderness, generosity, sympathy, understanding which are the living out of the principles of kindness. And it comes in unexpected ways.

I ask Stephen if he finds it hard to receive kindness; how does kindness appear in unexpected ways in his life? I discover that Stephen likes to tell stories, he is a good storyteller.

I could tell you a little story of a wonderful act of kindness I received in a very unexpected way earlier this year. Like bishops do, I go into schools quite a lot, and there's often Q&As with the children, and, to be honest, the questions are very predictable. Most of the time, you get the same old questions, you know ... 'What exactly do you do?' 'How much do you earn?' 'What's your favourite football team?' 'Who made God?' It's a range of questions, but reasonably predictable. And I love going into the schools, and this was with a primary school, 6- or 7-year-olds. So, when I'm asked the question, 'So what exactly do you do, Archbishop?' My answer is, 'Well, I'm the vicar for the vicars', because usually the local priest is in the room, so it's a nice nod to them. I said, 'Reverend so-and-so comes into your school every week, I'm just here, on a one-off, but who looks after Reverend so-and-so? Well, I said, that's my job. I'm the vicar for the vicars.'

Anyway, one little boy then puts up his hand – and bear in mind, for me, this has been quite a tough year – and this little boy puts up his hand and says, 'Archbishop, who looks after you?'

Just this little boy asking the question, just having the sensitivity to ask me, 'Who looks after you, who cares for you, Archbishop?' was an act of kindness. Because it was born out of this natural, instinctive, sympathy and understanding for another human being; to get inside the circumstance of another human being. So that I felt ministered to simply by him asking the question.

There is a warmth and a moment of vulnerability in this story that is profoundly touching. I know exactly what Stephen means by being ministered to by the innocence of a kindness offered without any judgement. A genuine question that expressed concern for the well-being of another person. There is an interesting shift of power in this exchange – a child ministering to a grown-up who had articulated his authority over another grown-up. Children notice these sorts of things. Jesus knew the importance of coming to God with the heart and kindness of a child. This isn't simply about innocence, this is about the openness of youth that is not encumbered by power dynamics or fear. When we come to God like a child, we arrive undaunted by status, we come loved and cherished. A child can ask powerful questions of adults, a childlike Christian can ask formidable questions of God.

Power dynamics are a significant challenge to kindness. An act of kindness from a child is a very different thing to a kindness from an archbishop. I press the question of power dynamics. Stephen replies:

> I'm aware of what you might call the power role that I have. So when I say thank you to someone it has a currency that other people's thank yous, though still lovely, don't have. Therefore, I think those of us who have agency, influence, authority and power, we have a special responsibility to act kindly. Because when we intentionally act kindly it has a value which far exceeds the few little words we're saying.

I ask Stephen if he thinks God is kind. I haven't asked everyone this question; it's not on my list. But the question has emerged when I become aware of the vulnerability of human kindness in relation to the 'wideness of God's mercy'. I sense that there is a vulnerability in Stephen's offering and receiving of kindness:

> Yes, God is kind. Because God is both the one who comforts us when we are afflicted, but also who challenges us and shows us the truth about ourselves. So sometimes God's kindness can be deeply, deeply uncomfortable; and sometimes we will reject it, because we are so in love with our own self-image that we don't want to see ourselves that clearly. I'm thinking about spiritual direction here. All the great spiritual writers say that the first step in the spiritual journey is the unmasking of illusion: to see the truth about yourself, and to have that revealed about yourself by God is a particular blessing. I think it is an act of loving-kindness.

Unmasking of illusion about oneself is a profound vulnerability that requires a particular sort of courage. But this is a private work of God, something that we rarely discuss or open to public scrutiny. So I ask Stephen who he receives kindness from, who is the kindest person he knows. There is a pause. An empty moment. And then the Archbishop answers, 'Oh, goodness, you floored me there, Ellen. So ... my grandson comes to mind.'

I know his grandson (his dad – Stephen's son Joe – and I work together). This child has been kind enough to drink cold orange squash from a china tea cup and humoured me that it was a 'nice cup of tea'; he has also spent over half an hour throwing the ball for my dog Tig, just because it was hilarious and Tig liked it. Stephen explains why he thinks his grandson is kind:

> I'm his granddad. He's my grandson ... I still sometimes replay in my head, was it last summer or even the summer before, when they were round? He was just playing and doing stuff, and he suddenly came and jumped on my lap and said, 'Oh, Papa, I love you.' He gave me a big hug, and it was, you know, it was just fantastic ... just utterly fantastic.

Sometimes remembering that just being alive, being loved, being 'Papa' is a wonderful kindness. At the end of the day, whatever our jobs, whoever we are, however much power we hold, we are humans in search of kindness. Humans made in the image of God who can offer and receive such wonderful gifts.[3]

47

The good container

Molly Boot, curate

30 October 2025

> 'There is no charm equal to tenderness of heart,' said she afterwards to herself. 'There is nothing to be compared to it. Warmth and tenderness of heart, with an affectionate, open manner, will beat all the clearness of head in the world, for attraction, I am sure it will.'
>
> *Jane Austen,* Emma[1]

Molly Boot (they/them) is a Church of England curate in Gloucestershire; they are a trustee of Greenbelt festival, theologian and musician. Molly begins their kindness conversation with an observation about the necessity for personal kindness, particularly when it comes to setting parameters around ministry:

> One of the big learnings that I've had to do over the last couple of years, especially entering ordained ministry, is having good boundaries because I was a bit of a kind of boundaryless blob for a very long time. I think I thought that that was what kindness had to look like, being very malleable and generous with my time and energy and resources and love and attention. But I used to be quite an uncritically vulnerable sort of person. The cost to my sense of self and well-being. I don't think I had a very strong sense of my own identity. I was just quite happy to go full-on people-pleaser and be whoever anyone needed me to be at any particular time.
>
> I think kindness is still that generosity but with good containers, with good boundaries that mean that I am able to be kind to myself while also being kind to others.

Molly's honesty and ability to reflect on past learning that has led to self-kindness is striking. This has enabled them to build resilience as well as kindness stamina. I am interested in their technique: 'Knowing what that costs – it's not avoiding the cost – but being quite aware of that and not ignoring or playing that down.' I can see that Molly has taken time to consider their capacity and priorities. They turn their phone off on days off, don't check emails and take annual leave. Molly must find time to 'switch off completely. And running, doing all of the things that make me feel like a full human being.' Molly refers to it 'as a sort of healthy selfishness – a more sustainable way of existing'. They tell me that their autism diagnosis has helped understand the need for containers, as has the therapy that they have received since 2018. They have also found themselves grounded by ministry, being comfortable with their sexuality and identity. 'Being in an inclusive church, where actually being out is not only OK, but is a gift, and is part of the outreach of the church, is absolutely mind-blowing.'

I am interested in how priestly ministry has impacted their containers: what new containers are there now?

> I think the Eucharist is the ultimate moment of letting someone else fill that for you. You can turn up to church, be completely knackered, desolate, grumpy, feeling the darkness and the crap of the world. But now, as a priest, being at the altar, breaking bread – that's the ultimate. Jesus has borne that in his body for us, for the whole of time. That is an extraordinary kindness ... It's so completely unpretentious.

Molly takes a pause ... then there is a moment of realization, a discovery: 'So ... thinking about the conversation so far, maybe the Eucharist is the container.' They excitedly continue, like a guiser gushing an idea:

> I wonder whether that's also my ethic of kindness, that the container of the liturgy, the container of the Eucharist, and the container of living sacramentality, that is being human, and in particular, for me, being a priest! Maybe that's the container, that vulnerability can be done in a way that is good and makes for flourishing. And that is generous without being detrimental to your own sense of self and well-being because there is this sacramental kind of space in which it's held.

It is a wonderful thing to see a new idea being born, a self-discovery being made, and a fresh insight emerging. We are both excited at Molly's kindness breakthrough: the Eucharist is the good container.

48

Feeling safe

Steve Chalke, founder, Oasis Charitable Trust

30 October 2025

> God is still in the very slow process of disenchanting us out of our love of winning and succeeding. The slow metamorphosis of our notions of God – from lion to lamb, from anger to tears, from lonely solitude to grateful community – is quietly taking place.
>
> *Richard Rohr*[1]

Steve Chalke is founder of the Oasis Charitable Trust;[2] he is a Baptist minister, writer and social justice activist. Steve considers his wife Cornelia to be the kindest person he knows:

> She sees colour, she's a great artist. She's quite extraordinary. She'll say to me, 'Do you remember what we did for our nineteenth wedding anniversary?' 'Do you remember what you were wearing?' I think, 'No! I have no idea!' Cornelia remembers – kindness is genuinely seeing the other feeling heard and feel safe in their presence.

Emotional safety is an important feature of the work of Oasis and a priority for Steve. Creating safe environments and offering stability is a kindness priority. Whether this is in the schools the trust oversees, in youth work, the farm or any community engagement, offering emotional and spiritual safety is paramount. Steve tells me of a recent encounter with a young person in one of the Oasis projects:

> Much of the work that Oasis does is with young people and adults who've never been loved or felt loved, never been seen, and never felt secure. We run a project called Oasis Restore, where a court can send a

young person to us for violent crime, rather than to a youth jail. So they are sentenced by the courts to be with us in a very secure environment.

As I sit and talk with these young people who've all committed very serious crime, what I discover is that every one of them is longing for a sense of safety, a sense of security, and what they hunger for is love. They hunger for somebody who will spend time with them, just because you choose to spend time with them.

Some months ago, back in the summer, I went down to Oasis Restore for a Saturday. I sat chatting with some of these kids. Then I said, 'Why don't we go play football?' We spent, I don't know, two and a half hours playing five-a-side football together. Then I suggested, 'Let's go play pool.' We played pool for ages. In the evening we watched a film together about Nelson Mandela. It was a BBC documentary about how Nelson had spent 16 years in solitary confinement on Robben Island. About how he'd arrived there an angry person but left as a world leader. Then we sat and talked about all this, and one kid says to me, one young man says to me after it all, 'Steve ... Will you be my dad?'

It seemed to me that Steve told me this story to demonstrate the many layers of kindness. There was his kindness at offering his free time to this project, then staying all day engaging these young people in various activities. There is also the kindness offered by the project itself – a project enabling an otherwise hard punishment to be softer and more reconciliatory. The final, and probably the most movingly impactful kindness, was offered by the young person who leaned out of his comfort zone to say something that left him vulnerable. That young person showed kindness to Steve who in that moment, recognizing the openness and vulnerability shown to him, both received and accepted it. I say the final, but perhaps there is another layer in the story being told – another kindness in me now recording it. Because now the layers of kindness are known by you and me. And that kindness inspires us to more kindness. And so the story continues.

It is obvious to me that Steve's faith inspires him to enact kindness, but I want to know what keeps that faith firm: how does he maintain kindness in a world where other priorities compete for space? Steve replies:

Jesus said, go the extra mile, turn the other cheek, surrender yourself. And he put his teaching into action. He went the extra mile. He gave himself. He surrendered himself. When I reflect on the cross and the resurrection, I think, 'What does the cross mean?' It means, the God of love is telling me, 'You can afford to walk this way, Steve. You can afford to live this life. You don't have to fight for status. You can afford to give yourself. You can afford to keep giving yourself. Because even if they end up crucifying you there's resurrection.'

Steve concludes our kindness conversation with this reflection:

> The universe is about love, because God is love. We're joining in. We're getting the rhythm. We're getting the beat. Getting aligned. Getting attuned. And that's a lifelong journey.

49

Campaigning with kindness

The Corbett Family

31 October 2025

> Jesus gave the disciples a formula for action, 'Be therefore wise as serpents and harmless as doves.' We must combine the toughness of the serpent and the softness of the dove, a tough mind and a tender heart.
>
> *Martin Luther King Jr*[1]

I met with four of the Corbett family for our kindness conversation on a rather gloomy Halloween, the night before All Souls. Henry has recently retired from serving as a priest in Everton in the north end of the City of Liverpool; Jane is a City Councillor for the Everton West Ward. Their eldest Emma is a social worker, and her sister Sarah is the founder of the Craftivist Collective.[2] I served my curacy from 2008 to 2011 as Henry's colleague at St John Chrysostom and St Peter's churches in Everton. Henry was an inspiring training incumbent and mentor, and working with him was an adventure and a privilege. It was Henry[3] who helped me understand the complexities of working in an urban setting and how to live a purposeful priestly life in a parish of high economic deprivation. Henry also introduced me to our beloved Everton Football Club – the team that breaks my heart as much as it makes it sing! Individually the Corbetts inspire, collectively they are a force! Here they address the question of kindness in the context of campaigning against injustices.

It is Jane who introduces the phrase 'deep positive humanity' to describe kindness – this resonates with all of us. They insist that kindness is not soft or naive. It is not just nice or an optional extra. For them it is a form of soft power,[4] and to be effective it must be thoughtful, contextual and empathetic. Sarah takes up this last point:

> It's important to acknowledge from the beginning of any protest that it is hard work for anyone to change their heart, mind, behaviour, policy or law, whether they are a politician, a business leader, or your neighbour who said something xenophobic. Campaigning can come across as unkind: you tell people, 'You're a bad person. You're wrong. Shame on you.' We forget to put ourselves in their shoes, to think about how they will receive our message. Threading kindness through protest is disarming rather than divisive, and can lead to collaboration or at least connection, and can mitigate risk of further polarization.

Our conversation moves to the practice of kindness. Emma says that sometimes working on maintaining kindness consistently requires discipline, and countering unkindness with kind exploration and explanation is a wise response:

> The journey to kindness sometimes starts with being honest that it's OK that your first reaction to an unkind comment or situation may be frustration and anger. The more you practise kindness, as with any muscle, the more you stretch, the easier it becomes. I remember the community newspaper Dad produced (*The Everton Telegraph*[5]) taking trouble to set out some of the facts about the asylum seekers who had come to our community because people didn't know the facts. You could jump in and say, you're this, you're that, but kindness is saying, hang on ... let's share some of the context kindly.

Jane agreed and pointed out that this was a response to a local issue fuelled by kindness, not a reaction fuelled by frustration. At this point there was excitement in the discussion and a wonderful sense of solidarity. Sarah chipped in: 'Yes, starting from good faith in people rather than bad faith.' Jane replied:

> Yes, and then suddenly it's a different place, and my shoulders go down, my brain starts to think better. When we're under pressure we sometimes have to respond quite quickly. But we need to do both short-term and long-term thinking. If I'm fuelling my response with kindness to people I disagree with, then that is a much more positive place for everyone involved. We can sit back, listen and understand each other.

This is what it means to respond with deep positive humanity – listening, creating space for discussion and really hearing the voices of the people involved. In this context of community cohesion, kindness looks to the long-term relationships, not just the short-term interactions, and is all the more effective for that. Kindness doesn't burn bridges. The door is always open for people to reach out with questions or curiosity rather than feeling they are being judged and 'othered', which creates disconnection. Jesus saying 'Love your enemies' is practical, kind and effective. It doesn't mean you love what they did or are doing, but you don't give up on them or label them, and in a community campaign that is vital to not causing more conflict.

This family has seen real social change happen. They have been involved in many campaigns, including saving houses, getting a new health centre, bridging sectarian divides, and the campaign to stop a group of asylum seekers being ill-treated in two local tower blocks perhaps best illustrates the effective role of kindness. Henry reflects:

> It started with friendly, kind visits to the asylum seekers with our community newspaper. Their backstories were listened to and understood. It continued with working with others, including the local MP, the police, the churches, the youth club. The campaign refused to disrespect either the asylum seekers or the authorities. It was a campaign that chose love and kindness, and it persevered and won.

Working alongside others in the Everton community influenced the Corbetts and powered their passion for kindness in their campaigns: Matt, Ann, Kathy, Frank, John, many others had so much local wisdom, treated everyone on the level, and would speak truth to power lovingly. Prayer and liberation theology fed the Corbetts' faith. A family trip to South Africa in 1991 for Henry's sabbatical taught them to view kindness as strategic and purposeful and as a vital antidote to revenge and violence. Nelson Mandela embraced kindness instead of retaliation, and the vision of a 'rainbow nation' was both brilliantly kind and so important for the future of the country.

The Corbett family all agree that kindness should be essential in their life and work. Sarah talked about her burning out as an activist and doubting the effectiveness of unkind protests – the Craftivist Collective was formed as a direct response to this burnout as she sought more gentle, kind and less aggressive ways to protest. Emma spoke about her work showing kindness to children in care and their networks. Henry speaks of the importance of kind encouragement as he helps out at churches in Toxteth and South Liverpool, and Jane speaks about the need to be as 'wise as a serpent and innocent as a dove'[6] and to have 'a tough mind and tender heart'.[7]

There is so much more I could write about what Sarah describes as our lovely collective Corbett community. But I will leave the last word to Jane:

> God loves the world! So, looking at the community that I represent, I know that God loves Everton. Deeply. Unconditionally. And that's something very powerful: every person made in the image of God. And all nations will be in heaven. That's a good future, isn't it? A heaven open to all, on offer to all. That should keep us kind.

50

Justice without kindness isn't justice

The students of St Margaret's Church of England Academy

4 November 2025

> For things to change we must dare to embrace altruism. Dare to say that real altruism exists, that it can be cultivated by every one of us, and that the evolution of cultures can favour its expansion. Dare, too, to teach it in schools as a precious tool for allowing children to realize their natural potential for kindness and co-operation ... Dare to take the fate of future generations seriously ... Dare to proclaim that altruism is not a luxury, but a necessity.
>
> *Matthieu Ricard*[1]

St Margaret's is one of the Diocese of Liverpool High Schools, part of the All Saints Multi Academy Trust. It is a boys' school that includes girls at sixth form. I am meeting a group of boys in the lower sixth, but I have got the time mixed up and arrive very early. Nevertheless, I am greeted fondly by the head of year who takes me in to see the head teacher and then into the staff room where I see an old friend and we have a chat. I am impressed by the informal and yet well-ordered arrangement of the school. Students and staff smile at me as I walk through the corridors, the school has a warmth and openness that enables me to feel relaxed and more confident. When I get to the classroom one of the boys makes me a cup of tea and offers me a biscuit. The kindness vibe is going very well.

I must admit I was a bit nervous about chatting to a group of sixth-form boys. I imagined a surly bunch of lads who were finding ways to get me to say something rude. But these were the kindest group of young people I'd met for a long time. They had a good grasp of ethics and had been learning about the Hebrew word *hesed* in religious education. As we started to talk about kindness, their ideas were articulate and engaging. They tell me that kindness means:

> Genuine care and gratitude for someone and wanting to go out of your way for someone.
> Respect and upholding human morals.
> Helping others, not neglecting others.
> Generosity.
> Trying to have a positive impact.
> Comforting, putting others before yourself.

The boys tell me that kindness feels: 'soft', 'nice', 'warm', 'powerful', 'it's a feeling that hears', 'soothing and calming', 'I wouldn't touch kindness, I'd hug it'. They can't agree on the colour of kindness and describe it variously as pink, yellow, white, light blue, green.

The boys clearly value kindness. I was moved by their accounts of when they had experienced kindness: 'My father sacrifices for me and the family despite it hindering his career'; 'My mum – she looks after me, she really cares'; 'My friend Steven is always open to talk, he's gentle natured and wise'; 'My old English teacher, through both actions and mannerisms, he always comes to lessons with a smile on his face'; 'My brother always goes out of his way to help.'

They had a strong sense of justice and felt kindness was integral. One boy insisted that 'justice without kindness isn't justice'.

These boys impressed me a great deal; they were witty and engaging. I found the way they listened to each other moving. The teachers, the support staff and the students all demonstrated kindness not just as an action but as a way of being with each other: the hospitality and the opening of doors, the waiting for each other to speak and really listening, being surprised and interested in each other's responses, offering encouragement and speaking highly of each other. These are instinctive kindness responses that are obviously valued and nurtured in this school. I came away feeling restored. If this is the future of kindness, it is hopeful.

51

Dancing in the kitchen

James Green, CEO Together Liverpool

4 November 2025

> Together Liverpool is working to build a kinder, more just and inclusive society through our Network of Kindness.
>
> *Together Liverpool*[1]

James is the CEO of Together Liverpool; I am chair of the charity. James leads the Network of Kindness – the members of this network are charities, churches and individuals who are engaging in social action. Most of these will be Anglican but Together Liverpool is ecumenical and has an increasing interfaith profile. The nature of our work means that we often talk about kindness and justice. However, this is the first time that we have interrogated kindness with such focus. James frames kindness in relation to love:

> If love is the feeling, then kindness is the practical application of it. And by practical, I don't just mean that you do something, but it's about the way that you are, the space that you create around yourself. So, it's your way of being in the world.

He views 'love as the engine that drives the kindness car'. Love fuels the momentum for social change where kindness is required to engage people. Justice is the 'striving for everyone having the opportunity to flourish', which implies a common good kindness where we each have a place to be the best we can be without being at the expense of another. Kindness is something we feel deeply, instinctively and vulnerably. While kindness is functional it is also an expression of the fullness of love that can be beyond reason and practicality.

James reflects on his experience of profound ordinary kindness particularly within a domestic context. James and his wife Alice foster children

– when a long-term placement ended it was painful and remains a source of sadness.

> The kindest thing we ever did for the children we fostered is we were always the same. So, you can throw us whichever way you want, but we'll always bounce back in a predictable pattern ... you know what you get from us, and ... it's not always easy to be consistent, is it? But I think that's one of the kindest things that you can be for a person.

This is my experience of James's kindness – I always know where I am with him. He is consistent and clear. I see this in his relationships with colleagues and with the people on the ground leading social action in parishes. Kindness is at the forefront of his practice and, as such, kindness is expected and the norm. So when James speaks of the kindness of his brother-in-law – who without being asked assisted with the trip to drop the foster children off for the last time and brought James and Alice back for a meal to help decompress – it is both profound and ordinary: 'He was kind and consistent and practical. He created the emotional safety and the space.'

James reminds me of my kindness. I almost want to reply, 'But of course ... isn't kindness what we have come to expect of each other?' As a team we have created an environment of kindness, a safe place for the vulnerability that kindness exposes. I might be the leader of that, but it has been a work of all of us to maintain and nurture it in our working practice. Something that I can see James holds as precious as I do. What a great privilege to work with colleagues who value kindness above status, ego and self-interest.

The way James speaks of kindness is as natural and ordinary as dancing with his daughter:

> It's funny, isn't it? Because there are some things that you just think should be entry-level that are really kind. Like, I play with my kids and that's not every child's experience of growing up. In terms of the impact that has on our daughter, that's huge. And so, the thing that you're creating in your home matters. We dance at home in the kitchen, and we're very silly, she has an expectation that that's what she finds, so she knows if she asks, can she dance? So, we are delighted to put the music on and dance ... There are set-piece moments that feel kind, but the everyday is more transformative, isn't it?

Perhaps we over-complicate kindness – when really its easy. It is like dancing in the kitchen with someone you love ... just because you can.

52

No spare people

Mark Russell, CEO, The Children's Society

11 November 2025

> … every child deserves to feel hopeful, happy and excited for their future.
>
> *The Children's Society*[1]

Mark Russell is CEO of The Children's Society; he has served as a lay member of the Synod of the Church of England and sat on the Archbishops' Council. Mark attributed the title of this kindness story to Rowan Williams – it became a central theme of our conversation and is pivotal to my understanding of Mark's approach to kindness.

> Kindness really matters to me. As Maya Angelou says, 'People forget what you say, but nobody forgets how you make them feel' … and I want people to feel better about themselves, and to feel that they matter. Kindness is about warmth, it's about care, it's about thoughtfulness. It's about generosity. It's about grace. It's about love. And in this organization, we've got kindness in our 'behaviours', and I've pushed hard for that to be included. Because I think it really matters in an organization as complicated and big as this, that we are a kind organization, and a caring organization.

Mark is adamant that a 'culture of kindness' is possible. He believes The Children's Society is an example of a kind organization – a place where this behaviour is expected and experienced. He sees this in all areas – from the volunteers in their shops to his direct reports. The structure he has fostered is one that has normalized kindness as a countercultural movement for social change. In an organization that puts children at its centre, kindness has become an ethical choice to ensure that 'every child matters';[2] it strives to place dignity and respect at the heart of their collective endeavours. I ask what inspires him personally to this calling:

> It's rooted in my faith. The heart of Jesus' ministry was the ministry to the edge, and to the margins, and to the people others looked down on, and others judged. He finds ways to include those people. And to bless them. The woman at the well – the way he ministered to her; the woman who was caught in adultery – he said, whoever's without sin throw the first stone, and they walked away. At least in the first century, people listening to him had the decency to walk away and put the stones down, whereas I think sometimes in our modern Church, we pick up the stones and throw them.

Mark has a strong sense of his calling as a leader who sets a kindness culture; he has a strong presence (even on a Zoom call), he offers reassurance, calm and hope. In a world that often feels hopeless it is encouraging to know that there are confident leaders such as Mark, leaders who value kindness above institutional benefit. When we hear so much about fiscally driven management systems it is hopeful that there are still CEOs who go out of their way to visit volunteers who have served diligently for 25 years, who send thank you cards to colleagues and who remember birthdays. It is touching that senior leaders such as Mark also appreciate the kindness shown to them. Mark tells me about Peggy who wrote encouraging letters and prayed for him when he worked at the Church Army, and he is grateful to Children's Society colleagues who have cared for him in recent times as he suffered three family bereavements. These may seem little things, but they are the ordinary kindnesses that humanize, show respect and value the person in the workplace.

If we believe (as Catholic social teaching tells us[3]) that the dignity of work is to be protected, then why shouldn't that dignity also include the right to kindness (as well as the right to productive work, to decent and fair wages, to the organization and joining of unions, to private property, and to economic initiative)? What if we collectively placed a higher value on kindness then we do financial profit? Mark asks the question of the Church as well as his own organization: 'What kind of organization do we want to be known as?'

> There's a huge high level of angst and stress in our society. And then you add into that the rise of the far right – what literally feels like our country is in two halves. You add into that the wider world, and what's going on in the Middle East, and what's going on in China and America.

> And people feel under a huge deal of strain. I think our job as a church is to say, 'What's our response to that?' Our response to that, I believe, passionately, is to be a kindness movement. A generosity movement, and a grace movement, and a love movement. That tells people you matter. Because ultimately, you matter to God. And your life matters.

Mark talks with an urgency – a sense that we need to grasp this opportunity as a church, as a community, as a people who love God. No matter our differences, the thing we can share is love and commitment to kindness. Somehow this doesn't seem fanciful when Mark calls out for it. When Mark calls for this sort of kindness it sounds like justice – a joyful connected movement for social change that places kindness at the forefront of our life together. Where nobody gets left out of kindness because there are no spare people.

53

No tapping out

Steven Horne, curate

13 November 2025

Service to others is the rent you pay for your room here on Earth.

Muhammad Ali

Steven is a curate in Ashford in Kent; he is the author of *Gypsies and Jesus*.[1] Steven is sitting at his desk in the home he shares with his wife and children. Behind him are his winning wrestling belts and various books, including his own excellent book about Traveller theology. Steven offered the Liverpool Cathedral Micah Social Justice Lecture a few years ago and as such we have spent time in the past speaking about his commitment to social action, theology at the margins and Holy Spirit-led ministry. So it comes as no surprise that this imbues his thinking about kindness:

> I've just tried to draw God into every aspect in every situation. It all stems back to my mum's increasing and growing fervent faith that was very Spirit-led. [It] led me to not in any way question God, to question the supernatural. It was done with a proper childlikeness of understanding God – I was never doubting those experiences. That really shaped my perspective. I started understanding that God was involved in everything that I was doing. It didn't mean that everything I was doing was godly, but everything I was doing, God was there. So, from the outset, kindness meant to me walking that walk of faith, and more an understanding rather than a verb.

It is this deep lived-out experience of God that is what draws me to Steven and his sense of kindness. He is spiritual in a real-life down-to-earth sort of way. He is unafraid of expressing his feelings and willing to speak freely of his fears and expectations. Yet he's also aware that the way he looks (shaved head, tattoos, grey hooded top) can mark him out as the sort of man who might fight his way out of a situation rather than feel it. Certainly, his wrestling belts and gym habits skill him to do that, but his natural inclination is to pray and listen to God. What he has heard is that he is loved and cherished, that God's 'undeserved grace, God's kindness' holds him and enables him to live a life that draws others into that ever-expanding grace.

He has recently begun a chaplaincy at a local gym and has found that this is a much-needed ministry to those who wouldn't usually connect with God or church. He considers introducing people to Jesus as the way he shows kindness. This love from God is the greatest kindness he has experienced, and he is determined to share it with others.

> Kindness in its more undiluted form looks at that situation, says 'OK, well, forget whether I want anything from this or not. That's not in the question. That's not in this equation. I should be doing this because of the kindness that was shown to me, for God to introduce himself to me.'

For Steven this sense of kindness as an understanding of the love of God that is a 'fruit that will naturally grow on you' was handed down by his mother Sue (aka Little Lady Sue). Sue is a natural intercessor, praying constantly and fervently; she has volunteered at church for over 40 years and generously gives to those in need from her 'bag of bits'. She also has a deep spiritual calling and connection – as did her mother before her. Steven describes this calling as 'kingdom thinking and kindness devoid of selfishness'. His inheritance is spiritually rich, complex and wise, but also inherently practical, straightforward and joyous. Sue once explained that her motivation to kindness is 'because Jesus loves me, I love other people'.

Steven is an academic, a man with a doctorate and a published author, yet his ministry is that of a kind practitioner steeped in ordinary profound faithfulness and trust in the kindness of God. Steven and his mother and siblings have travelled a difficult life journey, but he insists that God's grace reigns over all – good and bad. He explains:

> I see a sense in God's creation, the injustice in fallen creation, through a spiritual lens. I see that corruption, that fallenness within the spiritual realm, and how it affects our culture, our politics and so many aspects of our life. My mission is to do my part to restore God's creation. That's the act of kindness – doing what I can to help creation be how it was intended, rather than how it's been corrupted. Whether that comes

through writing, or political action, or praying in houses where people are experiencing unwanted phenomena. I look at it from a spiritual sense. I've seen enough that keeps me grounded and keeps me humble. If the most beautiful angel in heaven could fall, then arrogance and pride would be the first thing stepping in. I know there is no tapping out.[2]

54

Allahu jamilun, yuhibbul jamal[1]

Adam Kelwick, Muslim chaplain

19 November 2025

> At a time when divisions too often dominate the headlines, we believe it is more important than ever to highlight the values we share of respect, kindness, justice, and a commitment to the common good.
>
> *Interfaith Network*[2]

Adam Kelwick works in various contexts in the Liverpool City Region as a Muslim chaplain. He is a community activist and international humanitarian aid worker who achieved national prominence when he brought out food to protestors who had gathered outside Abdullah Quilliam Mosque in Liverpool.[3] His spontaneous act of generosity was a kindness offered at a time when the region was mourning the death of three children during a brutal attack on a dance class in Southport.[4] The attack sparked rioting across the region and nation; it left libraries and public spaces burned out, mosques stoned, and police lines charged. Adam's open-handedness at a time when many hands were formed into fists was a glimpse of light in a time of deep darkness.

> When we had the protesters outside the mosque, I was very aware that me taking food over to the protesters could have been seen as some kind of 'I'm better than you' act, and I have the moral high ground. People have said to me, 'You killed them with kindness, didn't you?' And I said, 'No, no, I didn't kill anybody. My goal was to bring them to life with kindness.' Because they've got kindness inside them as well. Everybody has, and sometimes you just need to activate it. If I can be a part of activating that kindness, then I'm honoured to be able to do that ... and it's not about bringing people down who are different, and

> even opposing you, and even showing enmity towards you. It's about bringing them up, so you both rise ... so you both rise together.
>
> These characteristics of talking about kindness, mercy, humility – there can be two manifestations of them. One of them is an act in which you put effort into employing them. Which is good. It's good. But the higher or the loftier form of it is when it's within the person's nature, and it just naturally flows.

As Adam speaks of the mercy and kindness of Allah he does so with a language that is full of beauty – it is honoured with a grateful respect. He explains that, 'Whenever this kindness and gentleness is put into something, into any action, when it's mixed with this, it beautifies it. The gentler and the more kind an action is, the more beautiful it becomes in the sight of God.' And when it's taken away from it, it uglifies it. Adam explains that this is because the very nature of God is beauty (as the opening quote from a hadith states). The beauty of Allah inspires kindness and brings beauty to what otherwise might be a transaction.

Adam and I enjoy an extended conversation about angels, miracles, jinn, the devil, creation, self-discipline, despair, fasting, Mary's silence after Jesus' birth, and the sincerity of Joseph who even when down in the well experienced the mercy of God. Eventually we focus and I ask what got in the way of kindness. Adam identified weakness, arrogance, ego and lack of sincerity: 'If you're sincere, it doesn't matter what the circumstances might seem to be like, whether they're good, whether they're bad, whether they're positive, whether they're negative. If you're sincere, that's your guarantee.' I ask him what helps him to remain focused on kindness, and he describes his mentors, two 'wise old men'. It is profoundly moving:

> They're both people who've devoted their lives to serving others. They have an intense, deep, loving connection with the Qur'an and with the person of the Prophet Muhammad (peace and blessings be upon him). Very, very deep, deep connection and love. One of them lives in Fez in Morocco, and the other lives in Aden in Yemen. I don't often talk about them, publicly. Not everybody gets it, and their lives are just ... All of blessings. All of blessings ... They have one common trait – they have love and they have time for poor people and the ones who are not seen in normal circles to be of any benefit.
>
> I lived with one of these men in his house for some time, so I've seen how, every single day, Ellen, he gathers together whatever income has come to him and he rounds his family up, his son, his daughter and his

> wife, and he's saying, what do we need for the house? He gets his family together. What do you need? They tell him what he needs, and he gives them the money for that. And then the rest of his money – this is every day he does this, every day – the rest of his money ... he knows of all the poor, really struggling people in the area. The ones who aren't the type to ask others ... and he'll make sure that all their needs are covered, and he starts from scratch the day after.

These are determined justice-filled kindnesses that are ordinary yet profound, unceremonious and almost domesticated in their everyday routine. As we came to the end of our kindness conversation I shared some of my recent heartache and Adam offered comfort: 'Sometimes God's kindness comes to you in a way which is so subtle, you don't realize it until many years down the line.'

As-salamu alaykum.[5]

55

El rachum[1]

Ariel Abel, rabbi, solicitor and trade unionist

20 November 2025

'Do not press me to leave you
  or to turn back from following you!
Where you go, I will go;
  where you lodge, I will lodge;
your people shall be my people,
  and your God my God.
Where you die, I will die –
  there will I be buried.
May the LORD do thus and so to me,
  and more as well,
if even death parts me from you!'

Ruth 1.16–17

Ariel Abel is a rabbi, solicitor and trade unionist who lives and works in the north-west of England. Ariel is a busy man; he is a compassionate person who takes justice and kindness seriously. As a trade union representative, he has assisted colleagues from many faith traditions as they face challenges in their working environments. Ariel's experience as a solicitor, as well as the gravity of his standing as a rabbi, give him an expertise that is reassuring. He also takes his faith seriously, so I was keen to get his wisdom about *hesed*, Ariel explains:

> *Hesed* runs through relationships, it runs through relationship-making, it really runs through work relationships, it runs through filial piety. It runs through a lot of things, pretty much everything on the human level.

> *Hesed* is an attribute which also runs through everything that is among the humans, but it is also attributed to and with God.
>
> Spiritually speaking, Jews, to this day, appeal to the attribute of mercy, which is expressed as *hesed*, loving-kindness, mercy. They're appealing to this loving-kindness of God as an alternative to the attribute of strict judgement. The opposite of strict judgements, which may include the concept ... as we have it in English law, for example of equity. Equity also emerges from compassion, or loving-kindness. *Hesed*. Can *hesed* be translated as compassion? It's an element within it, yes. It presumes compassion in there, because otherwise, why would you be loving in your kindness to anybody if you didn't have any ... if you didn't have compassion for them, put it that way?

Ariel and I dig deeper into the compassionate nature of *hesed* and how this human attribute is an echo of the nature of God. In human terms the action of *hesed* is a replica of the nature of a merciful God who chooses loving kindness. But Ariel points out, 'Loving-kindness cannot trump justice.' God will always seek out justice ahead of the desire to offer *hesed*. So people should also act with similar intentions and diligence. Ariel continues: 'No matter how noble, even spiritually, a church or a synagogue can be there is no point at which that will excuse a fall guy suffering injustice, because God will always seek justice.'

I press on the point of God seeking justice and offering *hesed* and Ariel takes me back to the verse in Micah 6.8. Ariel explains that the Hebrew word used here is (דורש) *doresh* – we translate as 'requires'. He explains:

> I'm going to bring [it] much more sharply into focus, and I'm going to say the following thing – 'require' is correct, but *doresh* is more than that. *Doresh* is a word which is also used in English law in the context of being an inquiry, like a criminal inquiry – what does the Lord *investigate* 'into' you? What does God investigate you over?

This requirement is therefore not simply a hopeful request or a compulsion or even an obligation. It is far more rigorous than that – *doresh* is a thorough investigation of our intentions, actions and purpose when it comes to justice and kindness. We should expect God to do a forensic investigation – to seek out the truth. Our responsibility is to be able to give account for the justice required of us, the loving kindness we do and the humility with which we walk through life with God.

Our conversation is rich and expansive. We speak about the many places in the Hebrew Scripture where *hesed* is evident – God's loving kindness and the *hesed* of people. We eventually land on the book of Ruth:

> Kindness is played out in the book of Ruth. Boaz doing a kindness with a maidservant who comes completely divested of all her dignity, she's got nothing. In that society, if you weren't married, you didn't have any dignity. If you were a foreigner and not married, you were even worse. If you were from the people of Moab, it was worse still ... She would have been looked down on quite badly. So, Ruth is saying ... please do some loving-kindness for the relative that you had who was married to me! He doesn't really have to do anything here, but he does ... that's the story. The result, the outcome of this, of course, is the Davidic Lineage.

It is impossible to ignore the significance of *hesed* – loving-kindness. It is pivotal to the story of all Abrahamic faiths, not least because due to the acting out of *hesed* Ruth bore a child who was to shift the tectonic plates of injustice towards eternal redemption.

56

Living with kindness

Andi Oliver, chef and television broadcaster

10 December 2025

> When given the choice between being right or being kind choose kind.
>
> *R. J. Palacio*[1]

I ask Andi what music she would equate with kindness, and she immediately mentions Stevie Wonder, describing him as 'kindness musically personified'. Andi Oliver is a chef, broadcaster, writer; she was a singer in a post-punk band called Rip Rig + Panic, and she continues to be culturally driven by music and popular culture. Andi is a patron of a community growing and food initiative, Squash,[2] an organization close to my heart located in Toxteth, Liverpool.

Given Andi's love of music it is hardly surprising that our conversation features ideas about the sound of kindness. Andi and I have known each other for several years but until this conversation I haven't asked her directly about her faith. She tells me that she is 'not a religious person at all, but I think I have faith in the universe'. This reply doesn't surprise me, but I find it interesting that Andi often uses language of redemption and grace in the way she talks about the impact of kindness in her life. I know that she has faced challenges over the years and that at the tender age of 62 she is feeling settled in her body and content emotionally and just wants to get on with looking after her family:

> In the Caribbean, there's a phrase, it's 'drink your water, cream your skin, and mind your business' – so, I'm trying to drink my water, cream my skin and mind my 62-year-old business.

Andi describes kindness as a 'gentle armour', and as a way of being curious and asking questions that break open relationships. She is baffled by people who 'choose to be unkind', as it feels to her that this sort of negativity requires depleting energy to maintain. She believes she has inherited kindness from her mother Maria, who in turn inherited it from her mother. Maria, a former teacher, lives with Andi and continues to be a kindness influence; as Andi points out, 'It makes a massive difference living with kindness'. But life hasn't always been kind to Andi:

> I dealt with a lot of racism and anger and aggression when I was younger, and it made me very fighty. I used to fight a lot, and just getting through the world on a daily basis was quite tiring. You know, it's tiring to not be kind. But it is a big step taking the choice ... I try to step towards the light and kindness – to live in light.

I ask what helped her to step towards that light and to live with kindness. Andi points to a time when she and her best friend Nena Cherry[3] travelled to Sweden to stay with Nena's family:

> I met her family, her mum. I'd already met her dad, Don Cherry, who was this incredible jazz musician. Her mother, Moki Cherry, was this extraordinary artist. She used to do these huge light boxes and tapestries, and loads of record covers, and build sets. They taught me so much. There were two social and musical movements that taught me kindness. One of them was punk, and the other one was jazz. Neither of those would make sense to a lot of people because I think the perception of punk and the perception of jazz are about wildness, and maybe aggression. Though that's not what I found in either of those worlds. In the world of punk, I found acceptance of otherness. I found freedom to be myself. I found light at the top of the mountain. I found a path and a world full of people who heard what I had to say and listened to what I had to say, even if it was different to what they had to say. I found discourse. I found commonality. I found intellectual exchange; I found, cerebral and intellectual challenge, which I loved, and spiritual challenge. And I think that the world of jazz, which I was introduced to by the Cherry family, gave me the same thing. It gave me this gentle balm for my soul. It gave me a sort of musical universe that blew my mind and tapped into a musicality that I didn't know I had in myself. It's brought me succour ... it brought me redemption in extraordinary ways.

I relate to Andi's feeling that music brings redemption – a recovery and rebalancing of soul. And I am fascinated by her language of salvation. She continues:

> There were different kinds of beauty, spiritually, physically and socially; there were different kinds of talent, and different things to reach for. All these things that I hadn't had ... I couldn't find words for. I couldn't quite put my finger on, I couldn't understand why I was so unhappy, and why I was so lost. I mean, I literally was lost, but now it was found. It was amazing, and there was grace.

I know that kindness is a gift for all people, not just those who profess a faith. It isn't confined to religious people – indeed, I am fully aware that unkind Christians exist! I am also conscious that a sense of emotional rescue – salvation – comes to some people through other experiences. Andi explains that religion has hurt her, hurt people of colour, enslaved, confined and set rules. In Andi's case she feels that music, family and friendship saved her. It also brought her kindness and a purpose. It would be unkind to deny the power of such experience. It feels important to hear that kindness is indiscriminate, unconfined and free. Like the gift of love, it is extended in graceful abundance to all.

57

Beloved and chosen

Jane Williams, theologian and writer

11 December 2025

> The greatest kindness one can render to any man consists in leading him from error to truth.
>
> *Thomas Aquinas*

During these kindness conversations Jane Williams has been named by several people as a kind person. So it is a special privilege to meet her and hear her thoughts on the subject. Jane is a theologian, lecturer at St Mellitus Theological College[1] and writer; she is married to Rowan Williams, former Archbishop of Canterbury, and they have two children. Jane is awaiting the birth of a grandchild who is now a week late arriving, so there is an air of expectancy as we begin our conversation. We throw ourselves into the subject with vigour as Jane explains that kindness is a 'devastating attention that God pays us and requires us to pay to each other ... it's very uncomfortable a lot of the time'. She continues:

> I think it does mean trying to pay attention to what's in front of you, and particularly to the person in front of you. Not to assume that I know who they are or what they need, or what I should be offering them until I've paid attention. I think that comes from the kind of theological reflection that I do on the way God attends to us – that extraordinary freedom that God gives us to approach truthfully.
>
> I would call it kindness, because God does not need anything from us. God is ... God, and is God with or without us? And so the fact that we are not necessary but present means that we are beloved and chosen, and therefore everything God does with us, in us, for us ... is for our good. It is kind. For our benefit, not for God's.

Jane is unlocking another door of understanding kindness for me. It begins to sink in that God's kindness flows from a place of love. In human terms we might exchange kindness out of need or obligation, but kindness in glory language is a freedom to love and be loved without boundaries. God's kindness isn't without discipline, but any regulation occurs as a way of growing love and strengthening our connection with the eternal. It is a beautiful outworking of a deepening discipleship and a drawing closer to God in love.

> It is about how we grow up into the measure of the stature of the fullness of Christ. It's how we grow beyond needing milk into solid food, and it is about truthfulness; all the practices of Christian spiritual disciplines are about truthfulness. Knowing that we can dare to be truthful before God, because God's love towards us is never going to change, whatever. God already knows us, already loves us, absolutely, and therefore it is possible to be safe – not cosily safe, but personally and integrally safe in the presence of God and learning more and more about ourselves in that reality.
>
> God always gives us to each other as part of that kindness ... me on my own with God is a space where I can still be self-deceptive. Me on my own with God, and then God's people, is a place of learning. In order to understand God's kindness, I've got to reciprocate it. I've got to try and do for others what God does.

Jane talks of the relentlessness of God's love, and I express excitement and a little fear at the idea that God insists on kindness as a response to love. Jane explains: 'God's love that doesn't let us get away with things.' This love chases truth and reality gently but endlessly asking more of us, revealing more capacity for love.

God's kindness relates to God's longing for justice.

> Justice is not an abstract thing; it is the demonstration of the worth of people. In the Prophets and the Psalms God's justice is always, in a way, a threat to the kind of systems that we set up in the world, which are always systems that reinforce wealth and acquired power, and not to highlight the infinite worth of every person.

Human systems appear to be set up to encourage competition and individualism. Ours is a world where it is almost impossible simply to belong and be loved for who you are. God's glory, the coming kingdom, as signalled by the prophets and the psalmists, challenges this assertion. In

God's system we are not rivals and divided, we are eternally interconnected and powered by love. Perhaps kindness is a way to open ourselves up to this vision? Perhaps kindness itself can be a tool for the pursuit of the common good? Jane has this advice about how to find and propagate kindness:

> Seek out those you know who are deliberately kind. Foster those relationships where you can see somebody is willing to offer kindness and then try to simply do the same. The spiritual practices of the Christian tradition, if we took them seriously, would be hugely helpful: prayer and silence and confession. As Christians, we're very fortunate to have those sets of practices that are readily available.
>
> Notice the places that regularly trigger us to want to be unkind, notice the places where we've given ourselves permission to be snide or mean. Notice the way they diminish us. We are always as much the losers for our own unkindness. That makes us less than we long to be.

Conclusion

Believe in kindness

'They say Aslan is on the move – perhaps has already landed.'

And now a very curious thing happened. None of the children knew who Aslan was any more than you do; but the moment the Beaver had spoken these words everyone felt quite different. Perhaps it has sometimes happened to you in a dream that someone says something which you don't understand but in the dream it feels as if it has some enormous meaning – either a terrifying one which turns the whole dream into a nightmare or else a lovely meaning too lovely to put into words, which makes the dream so beautiful that you remember it all your life and are always wishing you could get into that dream again. It was like that now. At the name of Aslan each one of the children felt something jump in its inside. Edmund felt a sensation of mysterious horror. Peter felt suddenly brave and adventurous. Susan felt as if some delicious smell or some delightful strain of music had just floated by her. And Lucy got the feeling you have when you wake up in the morning and realize that it is the beginning of the holidays or the beginning of summer.

C. S. Lewis[1]

This book has been full of stories of kindness, we have heard from a rich pageant of people who have differing views about mercy, love, generosity and justice. In many ways this book is a hopeful celebration of how we would like life, the Church and the world to be. But for many of us this has not always been our experience of the Church or the faithful communities we trusted. Some of us have experienced profound unkindness in the Church, often more so than outside it. We have not seen people being their best selves or experienced consistency, rigour, appropriate professional distance or mercy. Some of us have been mistreated, abused and do not feel safe. We have been lied to or gossiped about, prayer has been weaponized and safeguarding inadequate. Some of us have been racially abused or sexualized; we have been marginalized because of our gender or sexuality, class and social standing has impacted our prospects; we have been pitied or overlooked because we do not meet zealous physical or educational standards, and our so-called disabilities have been marginalized or ridiculed as weakness. Of course, the Church, like any group of people, isn't immune to unkindness, but we need to do better. The tiniest drop of unkindness infects us all, and none of us are spared the pernicious ravages of its consequences. We cannot continue to tolerate unkindness. We must stop, repent, turn back and fall on the mercy of God. Making justice, kindness and humility our primary priority as the people of God would transform our contentious debates into conversations, and our disputes would no longer require a triumphant victory.

In his book *Humankind: A hopeful history*, Rutger Bregman makes a convincing case for the assertion that people are a lot kinder than we think. He argues that it is a myth that 'by their very nature humans are selfish, aggressive and quick to panic'.[2] He disagrees with the Dutch biologist Frans de Waal who describes our social constructs as fragile – what de Wall calls '*veneer theory*:[3] the notion that civilisation is nothing more than a thin veneer that will crack at the merest provocation'.[4] Bregman argues that when the chips are down, when bombs fall, crisis comes, pandemic hits, etc., instead of breaking 'we become our best selves'.[5] While he offers strong scientific and social evidence for this being the case, Bregman points out that 'it could be more of a reality if we believe it to be true'.[6] So let's be our best selves. Let's have faith in our ability to be kind.

Christians believe that Jesus conquered sin and death by his resurrection, that malevolent forces have been defeated and the struggle with evil is over. And yet we also seem to act as if this is a future glory not a victory to claim now. The gifts of the Spirit, freely given as a sign of our liberty, are not shared with glorious abandon in quite the way we'd expected. When we do talk of this freedom, we often describe it as something that belongs to a few of us – the select group who hold the truth – as if we are inside the cordon and the zombie apocalypse is happening in the nasty world beyond the walls of our imagined sanctuary. But there is no need for a sanctuary, because we don't need to hide. The veil has been torn in two.[7] We've got this! Because God has got this! There are no zombies, there are no bad people. There are just people who don't know they are good yet. Grace is just around the corner if there is enough light to see it. Perhaps the purpose of our faith is to shine light on the goodness and to love the parts of people that make the world a kinder place. The darkness has not overcome it.

We should be brave enough to live out our belief that our world is being transformed by a living God through Jesus, and that kindness is a reality that has been gifted to all people for all time. That people of faith are called to be like salt that gently, generously and lovingly flavours what God has already put in the pot. We don't need to do the stirring – loving parent God is the chef in this allegory. We don't need to turn up the gas – the Holy Spirit is the fire! (Perhaps I have stretched the metaphor too far ...)

This book has captured thoughts on kindness expressed by a few people in a short four-month period in 2025. This is the time to make kindness our present and our future. Kindness is on the move. Perhaps it has already landed. Please join Project Kindness in your own unique way and share your kindness story with a world that so desperately needs to hear it.

Floating around the internet is a parable of unknown origin. It contains what I believe is a simple but profound truth:

> An old man says to his grandson: 'There's a fight going on inside me. It's a terrible fight between two wolves. One is evil – angry, greedy, jealous, arrogant and cowardly. The other is good – peaceful, loving, kind, humble, generous, honest and trustworthy. These two wolves are also fighting within you, and inside every person too.'
>
> After a moment, the boy asks, 'Which wolf will win?'
>
> The old man smiles.
>
> 'The one you feed.'[8]

Bibliography

Arnold, Sarah Jane, 2018, *The Kindness Coach*, Michael O'Mara Books: London.

Bączyk-Bell, Charlie, 2024, *Queer Redemption: How queerness changes everything we know about Christianity*, Darton, Longman & Todd Ltd: London.

Bayes, Paul, 2019, *The Table: Knowing Jesus: Prayer, friendship, justice*, Darton, Longman & Todd: London.

Bessey, Sarah (ed.), 2021, *A Rhythm of Prayer: A collection of meditations for renewal*, SPCK: London.

Bessey, Sarah, 2024, *Field Notes for the Wilderness*, Convergent Books: New York.

Bregman, Rutger, 2020, *Humankind: A hopeful history*, Bloomsbury: London.

Brown, Brene, 2018, *Dare to Lead*, Penguin: London.

Butler-Gallie, Fergus, 2025, *Twelve Churches: An unlikely history of the buildings that made Christianity*, Hodder & Stoughton: London.

Cheng-Tozun, Dorcus, 2023, *Social Justice for the Sensitive Soul: How to change the world in quiet ways*, Broadleaf: Minneapolis, MN.

Cherry, Nena, 2025, *A Thousand Threads*, Vintage: London.

Coleman, Kate, 2021, *7 Deadly Sins of Women in Leadership: Overcome self-defeating behaviour in work and ministry*, Harper Christian Resources: London.

Coleman, Kate, 2024, *Metamorph: Transforming your Life and Leadership: Inspired wisdom from the extraordinary, ordinary people of the Bible*, 100 Movements Publishing: London.

De Waal, Frans, 2013, *The Bonobo and the Atheist: In search of humanism among the primates*, W. W. Norton & Company: New York.

Eberhard, Arnold, 1998, *Salt and Light*, Plough Publishing: New York.

Edman, Liz, 2016, *Queer Virtue: What LGBTQ people know about life and love and how it can revitalize Christianity*, Beacon Press: Boston, MA.

France-Williams, A. D. A., 2020, *Ghost Ship: Institutional Racism and the Church of England*, SCM Press: London.

Gale, Charlotte, 2024, *Simple, Generous, Open: Mission and renewal in the progressive church*, Canterbury Press: Norwich.

Goode, Tim, 2026, *Breaking, Not Broken: Ableism and the Church after Constantine*, SCM Press: London.

Hammond, Claudia, 2022, *The Keys to Kindness: How to be kinder to yourself, others and the world*, Canongate: Edinburgh.

Hays, Richard and Hays, Christopher, 2024, *The Widening of God's Mercy: Sexuality within the biblical story*, Yale University Press: New Haven, CT.

Held Evans, Rachel, 2018, *Inspired: Slaying giants, walking on water, and loving the Bible again*, Nelson Books: Nashville, TN.

Hersey, Tricia, 2024, *Rest is Resistance: Free yourself from grind culture and reclaim your life*, Aster: London.

Horne, Steven, 2022, *Gypsies and Jesus: A Traveller theology*, Darton, Longman & Todd: London.

Julian of Norwich, 2015, *Revelations of Divine Love*, Oxford University Press: Oxford.

King Jr, Martin Luther, 2017, *A Gift of Love: Sermons from strength to love*, Penguin Classics: London.

Kraft, Houston, 2020, *Deep Kindness: A Revolutionary Guide for the Way we Think, Talk, and Act in Kindness*, Simon Element: New York.

Lewis, C. S., 1950, *The Lion, the Witch and the Wardrobe*, Geoffrey Bles: London.

Mackay, Hugh, 2021, *The Kindness Revolution: How to restore hope, rebuild trust and inspire optimism*, Allen and Unwin: Crows Nest, NSW.

Malinowski, Bronisław, 2022, *Argonauts of the Western Pacific*, Must Have Books: London.

Manfredi, Jayne, 2024, *Waking the Women: Faith, menopause and the meaning of midlife*, Canterbury Press: Norwich.

Mauss, Marcel, 2001, *The Gift: The form and reason for exchange in archaic societies*, Routledge: London.

Percy, Emma, 2014, *What Clergy Do*, SPCK: London.

Peterson, Eugene, 2000, *Long Obedience in the Same Direction: Discipleship in an instant society*, Inter-Varsity Press: Downers Grove, IL.

Philips, Adam, and Taylor, Barbara, 2010, *On Kindness*, Penguin: London.

Poole, Eve, 2024, *Robot Souls; Programming humanity*, CRC Press: Oxford.

Poole, Martin, 2025, *Real Life Rev: A clergy survival guide*, Canterbury Press: Norwich.

Pope Francis, 2016, *The Name of God is Mercy, Pope Francis speaking to Andrea Tornielli*, Random House: London.

Portas, Mary, 2021, *Rebuild: How to thrive in the new kindness economy*, Penguin: London.

Ricard, Matthieu, 2013, *Altruism: The science and psychology of kindness*, Atlantic Books: London.

Rohr, Richard, 2025, *The Tears of Things: Prophetic wisdom for an age of outrage*, SPCK: London.

Rozin, P., Haidt, J. and McCauley, C. R. (2008), 'Disgust', in M. Lewis, J. M. Haviland-Jones and L. F. Barrett (eds), *Handbook of Emotions*, 3rd edn, The Guilford Press: New York.

Shakespeare, Steven, 2019, *The Earth Cries Glory: Daily prayer with creation*, Canterbury Press: Norwich.

Skinner, Mim, 2020, *Jailbirds/the Prison Teacher: Stories from Britian's most notorious women's prison*, Seven Dials: London.

Skinner, Mim, 2022, *Living Together: Searching for community in a fractured world*, Footnote: London.

Soskice, Janet, 2007, *The Kindness of God: Metaphor, gender, and religious language*, Oxford University Press: Oxford.

Summers, Nahla, 2019, *A Culture of Kindness: for leaders of the future*, self-published.

Testament, 2021, *Orpheus in the Record Shop and The Beatboxer*, Methuen: London.

Tolstoy, Leo, 1997, *A Calendar of Wisdom*, Hodder & Stoughton: London.

van der Kolk, Bessel, 2015, *The Body Keeps the Score: Brain, mind, and body in the healing of trauma*, Penguin: London.

Wells, Samuel, 2025, *Constructing an Incarnational Theology: A Christocentric view of God's purpose*, Cambridge University Press: Cambridge.

Wharton, Kate, 2013, *Single-Minded: Being single, whole and living life to the full*, Monarch: London.

Williams, Jane, 2018, *The Merciful Humility of God*, Bloomsbury: London.

Notes

Introduction

1 'Try a Little Kindness' is a song written by Curt Sapaugh and Bobby Austin, first recorded by American country music singer Glen Campbell.
2 The most useful history of kindness and definition can be found in Adam Philips and Barbara Taylor, 2010, *On Kindness*, Penguin: London.
3 The Sussex Centre for Research on Kindness, https://www.sussex.ac.uk/research/centres/kindness/, accessed 10.02.2026.
4 Mark and I had a radio show called *In the Pop Kitchen*. One of Mark's lockdown projects was to turn the show into a website that has links to all the shows and comments on the influences and choices of songs. You can read and listen at http://www.inthepopkitchen.com/, accessed 10.02.2026.
5 Sheldon Retreat in Devon, https://www.sheldonretreat.com/, accessed 10.02.2026.

Chapter 1: Jonathan Swales

1 Jon Swales, Cruciform Justice: Following Jesus towards justice, https://www.cruciformjustice.com/, accessed 10.02.2026.
2 Trinity College Bristol, https://www.trinitycollegebristol.ac.uk/, accessed 10.02.2026.
3 Lighthouse West Yorkshire, https://www.lighthousewestyorkshire.org.uk/, accessed 10.02.2026.

Chapter 2: David Hayward

1 Sarah Bessey, 2024, *Field Notes for the Wilderness*, New York: Convergent Books.
2 You can buy a copy (as I say, I have the original!) from The NakedPastor, https://nakedpastor.com/products/women-and-the-resurrection, accessed 10.02.2026.
3 The Lasting Supper, https://thelastingsupper.com/, accessed 10.02.2026.
4 The NakedPastor, https://nakedpastor.com/pages/about, accessed 10.02.2026.

Chapter 3: Adjoa Andoh

1 Fairtrade Foundation, https://fairtrade.net/uk-en.html, accessed 11.2.2026.
2 Tree Aid, https://www.treeaid.org/, accessed 11.2.2026.

Chapter 4: Winne Varghese

1 William Shakespeare, *The Merchant of Venice*, Act IV, scene I.

Chapter 5: Martin Poole

1 J. R. R. Tolkien, *The Hobbit*, HarperCollins: London.
2 Martin Poole, *Real Life Rev: A clergy survival guide*, Canterbury Press: Norwich.
3 Beyond, an initiative combining art in public spaces with Christian spirituality, www.beyondchurch.co.uk/, accessed 18.02.2026.
4 Places of Welcome, www.placesofwelcome.org.uk/, accessed 18.02.2026.

Chapter 6: Guy Hewitt

1 Guy Hewitt, *The Church of England, Faith in the City and Racial Justice: Addressing growing social polarisation*, https://williamtemplefoundation.org.uk/temple-tracts/, accessed 18.02.2026.
2 Queen Anne's Bounty, a predecessor fund of the Church Commissioners, had links (through investments it made and benefactions it received) with transatlantic chattel slavery. In response to this, the Church Commissioners have made a funding commitment of £100 million, to invest in a better future for all, working with and for communities affected by historic transatlantic slavery, with the intention that it creates a lasting legacy. https://www.churchofengland.org/sites/default/files/2024-03/project-spire_oversight-group-tors_v_5.pdf

Chapter 7: Ash Barker

1 Hugh Mackay, 2021, *The Kindness Revolution: How to restore hope, rebuild trust and inspire optimism*, Allen and Unwin: NSW Australia, p. 47.
2 Seedbeds, https://seedbeds.org/, accessed 19.02.2026.
3 Cooking with Poo & Friends, https://www.cookingwithpoo.com/, accessed 19.02.2026.
4 Anglican Communion, https://www.anglicancommunion.org/mission/marks-of-mission.aspx, accessed 19.02.2026.
5 Renowned civil rights leader and Christian community development pioneer.

Chapter 8: Richard Coles

1 Claudia Hammond, 2022, *The Keys to Kindness: How to be kinder to yourself, others and the world*, Canongate: Edinburgh, p. 29.

Chapter 9: Jayne Manfredi

1 Arnold Eberhard, 1998, *Salt and Light*, Plough Publishing: New York.
2 Jayne Manfredi, 2024, *Waking the Women: Faith, menopause and the meaning of midlife*, Canterbury Press: Norwich.

Chapter 10: Mim Skinner

1 Mim Skinner, 2020, *Jailbirds/the Prison Teacher: Stories from Britian's most notorious women's prison*, Seven Dials: London, p. 283.
2 Mim Skinner, https://www.mimskinner.co.uk/, accessed 20.02.2026.
3 Refuse, https://refusedurham.org.uk/ 'We REfUSE to be part of a wasteful food system. We work to Reduce, Rescue, and RE-USE, so that good food doesn't become Refuse'. Accessed 20.02.2026.

4 LDCSA, https://www.ldcsa.org.uk/annual-prison-lecture, accessed 20.02.2026.
5 Mim Skinner, https://www.mimskinner.co.uk/portfolio-collections/my-portfolio/jailbirds, accessed 20.02.2026.

Chapter 11: Charlie Bączyk-Bell

1 Pope Francis, 2016, *The Name of God is Mercy: Pope Francis speaking to Andrea Tornielli*, Random House: London.
2 Charlie Bączyk-Bell, 2024, *Queer Redemption: How queerness changes everything we know about Christianity*, Darton, Longman & Todd Ltd: London.
3 The Church of England, https://www.churchofengland.org/resources/living-love-and-faith, accessed 20.02.2026.

Chapter 12: Malcolm Chamberlain

1 Tom Wright suggests that the Bible is written in five acts: *creation*, *fall*, *Israel*, *Jesus* and *the Church*. He proposes that the fifth act is unfinished and heading towards a new creation – and as such it is the responsibility of the Church (by which he means the whole collection of Christian believers) to participate in the completion of the story. Christian people should do this by 'faithfully improvising' using the Scriptures as our inspiration.
2 Tom Wright, 2005, *Scripture and the Authority of God*, SPCK: London, p. 123.
3 There is not much internet evidence left of Dream's existence. This *Guardian* article offers a sense of its impact and playfulness: https://www.theguardian.com/commentisfree/belief/2009/apr/20/religion-christianity, accessed 20.02.2026.
4 I have tried to avoid technical terms; so, sorry I have slipped one in here. Basically, hermeneutic means interpretation of the Bible. Biblical scholars use it because there are various approaches to biblical interpretation, and this term is a good cover-all.

Chapter 13: Tim Goode

1 Tim Goode, 2026, *Breaking, Not Broken: Ableism and the Church after Constantine*, SCM Press: London.
2 Exodus 3.2–6.
3 Psalm 133.

Chapter 14: Kate Coleman and Cham Kaur-Mann

1 Tricia Hersey, 2024, *Rest is Resistance: Free yourself from grind culture and reclaim your life*, Aster: London, p. 45.
2 Next Leadership, https://www.nextleadership.co.uk/, accessed 20.02.2026.
3 Kate Coleman, 2021, *7 Deadly Sins of Women in Leadership: Overcome Self-Defeating Behaviour in Work and Ministry*, Harper Christian Resources: London.
4 Kate Coleman, 2024, *Metamorph: Transforming Your Life and Leadership: Inspired wisdom from the extraordinary, ordinary people of the Bible*, 100 Movements Publishing: London.
5 Hersey, *Rest is Resistance*, p. 38.
6 Hersey, *Rest is Resistance*, pp. 25–6.

Chapter 15: John Bell

1 John Bell, 1987, 'The Summons', Iona Community, GIA Publications.

Chapter 16: Jenny Sinclair

1 Together for the Common Good, https://togetherforthecommongood.co.uk/what-you-can-do/pray, accessed 20.02.2026.
2 Together for the Common Good, https://togetherforthecommongood.co.uk and https://t4cg.substack.com/, accessed 20.02.2026.
3 Together for the Common Good, https://togetherforthecommongood.co.uk/about/catholic-social-thought, accessed 20.02.2026.
4 *Age of Alienation: The collapse in community and belonging among young people, and how we should respond*, 2021, UK Onward, https://www.ukonward.com/wp-content/uploads/2021/09/Age-of-Alienation-Onward.pdf, accessed 20.02.2026.
5 P. Rozin, J. Haidt and C. R. McCauley, 2008, 'Disgust', in M. Lewis, J. M. Haviland-Jones and L. F. Barrett (eds), *Handbook of Emotions*, 3rd edn, The Guilford Press: New York, pp. 757–76.
6 Together Liverpool, https://togetherliverpool.org.uk/whats-new/towards-the-common-good-three-evenings/, accessed 20.02.2026.
7 Together for the Common Good, https://t4cg.substack.com/p/from-charity-to-solidarity-a-radical, accessed 20.02.2026.

Chapter 17: Liz Edman

1 Dorcus Cheng-Tozun, 2023, *Social Justice for the Sensitive Soul: How to change the world in quiet ways*, Broadleaf: Minneapolis, MN, p. 26.
2 Queer Virtue, https://www.queervirtue.com/, accessed 20.02.2026.
3 Liz Edman, 2016, *Queer Virtue: What LGBTQ People Know About Life and Love and How It Can Revitalize Christianity*, Beacon Press: Boston, MA.
4 Bessel van der Kolk, 2015, *The Body Keeps the Score: Brain, mind, and body in the healing of trauma*, Penguin: London.
5 Matthew 13.44.

Chapter 18: Andy Flannagan

1 *The Irish Times*, https://www.irishtimes.com/culture/tv-radio-web/trust-yourself-be-a-good-friend-bono-s-six-thoughts-for-sixth-class-1.4283235, accessed 20.02.2026.
2 *Independent*, https://www.independent.co.uk/news/uk/politics/hand-over-fist-the-red-hand-of-ulster-still-has-the-power-to-divide-northern-ireland-1950412.html, accessed 20.02.2026.
3 Corrymeela is a peace-building community based in Ballycastle, Northern Ireland. Founded in 1965, the organization has played a significant part in bringing different communities together to shape peace and security on the island of Ireland. Mark's family have been members of the community since its foundation: https://www.corrymeela.org/, accessed 20.02.2026
4 St Francis Xavier's Church, Liverpool, https://sfxchurchliverpool.co.uk/, accessed 20.02.2026.
5 Romans 14.17.

Chapter 19: Fergus Butler-Gallie

1 Fredrick William Faber, 'There's a Wideness in God's Mercy' (1892).
2 Fergus Butler-Gallie, 2025 *Twelve Churches: An unlikely history of the buildings that made Christianity*, Hodder & Stoughton: London.

Chapter 20: Testament

1 Testament, 2021, *Orpheus in the Record Shop and The Beatboxer*, Methuen: London.
2 Testament, https://www.testamenthomecut.com/, accessed 20.02.2026.

Chapter 21: Kate Bottley

1 'Hostess with the Mostest' is a song by Irving Berlin. It features in the musical *Call Me Madam* and was made famous by Ethel Merman who starred as Sally Adams in the musical and recorded it in 1953: Smule, https://www.smule.com/recording/call-me-madam-irving-berlin-ethel-merman-hostess-with-the-mostess/1044408391_3576575300, accessed 20.02.2026.
2 CEO and founder of GLAS group, GLAS, https://glasmethod.com/kindness, accessed 20.02.2026.
3 *The Guardian*, https://www.theguardian.com/world/2017/apr/11/protest-photos-the-power-of-one-woman-against-the-world, accessed 20.02.2026.

Chapter 22: Liz Hassall

1 Leo Tolstoy, 1997, *A Calendar of Wisdom*, Hodder & Stoughton: London, 7 January, p. 7.
2 Liz was inspired sometimes to be 'just good enough' by Emma Percy, 2014, *What Clergy Do*, SPCK: London.
3 Matthew 12.9–14; Luke 13.10–17; Mark 3.2–5; John 5.1–18.
4 John 8.1–11.

Chapter 23: Rob Wickham

1 Henri Nouwen, 2017, *Love, Henri: Letters on the spiritual life*, Hodder & Stoughton: London.
2 Church Urban Fund, https://cuf.org.uk/, accessed 20.02.2026.
3 Housing Justice, https://housingjustice.org.uk/, accessed 20.02.2026.
4 Together Liverpool, https://togetherliverpool.org.uk/, accessed 20.02.2026.
5 'There was a Levite from Cyprus, Joseph, to whom the apostles gave the name Barnabas (which means "son of encouragement")', Acts 4.36.
6 Hebrews 12.1.
7 The Daily Office, https://www.dailyoffice2019.com/commemorations/2aa3195f-eb1d-4628-b8f7-8a7b5da46c71, accessed 20.02.2026.

Chapter 24: Ravi Holy

1 Claudia Hammond, 2022, *The Keys to Kindness: How to be kinder to yourself, others and the world*, Canongate: Edinburgh, p. 223.

2 Christian Universalist Association, https://christianuniversalist.org/wp-content/uploads/2023/01/DamnedNonsense-RaviHoly.pdf, accessed 20.02.2026.
3 Heal for Life Foundation, https://healforlife.org.uk/, accessed 20.02.2026.
4 Find a Helpline, https://findahelpline.com/, accessed 20.02.2026.

Chapter 25: Charlotte Gale

1 Mary Portas, 2021, *How to Thrive in the New Kindness Economy*, Penguin: London.
2 St Clare's, https://stclaresatthecathedral.org/, accessed 20.02.2026.
3 Charlotte Gale, 2024, *Simple, Generous, Open: Mission and renewal in the progressive church*, Canterbury Press: Norwich.
4 Ciriec, https://ciriec.es/valencia2022/wp-content/uploads/COMUN-241.pdf, accessed 20.02.2026.
5 European Parliament, https://www.europarl.europa.eu/RegData/etudes/BRIE/2022/703349/IPOL_BRI(2022)703349_EN.pdf, accessed 20.02.2026.
6 GSEF, https://www.gsef-net.org/, accessed 20.02.2026.
7 Power to Change, https://www.powertochange.org.uk/, accessed 20.02.2026.

Chapter 26: Eve Poole

1 Eve Poole, 2024, *Robot Souls: Programming in humanity*, CRC Press: Oxford, p. 71.
2 Eve Poole, https://evepoole.com/, accessed 20.02.2026.
3 UK Legislation, https://www.legislation.gov.uk/ukcm/2021/2/contents, accessed 20.02.2026.

Chapter 27 Sam Wells

1 Claudia Hammond, 2022, *The Keys to Kindness: How to be kinder to yourself, others and the world*, Canongate: Edinburgh, p. 4.
2 Acts 10.24–33.
3 St Martin in the Fields, https://www.stmartin-in-the-fields.org/people/revd-dr-sam-wells/, accessed 20.02.2026.
4 Richard Hays and Christopher Hays, 2024, *The Widening of God's Mercy: Sexuality within the biblical story*, Yale University Press: New Haven, CT.
5 Samuel Wells, 2025, *Constructing an Incarnational Theology: A Christocentric view of God's purpose*, Cambridge University Press: Cambridge.

Chapter 28: Kate Wharton

1 Brene Brown, 2018, *Dare to Lead*, Penguin: London.
2 St Bart's, https://www.stbartholomewsroby.org.uk/, accessed 20.02.2026.
3 Kate Wharton, 2013, *Single-Minded: Being single, whole and living life to the full*, Monarch: London.
4 Single Friendly Church Network, https://www.singlefriendlychurch.com/, accessed 20.02.2026.
5 Paul Bayes, 2019, *The Table: Knowing Jesus: Prayer, friendship, justice*, Darton, Longman & Todd: London.
6 Jesus feeds the multitude: Matthew 14.13–21; Mark 6.31–44; Luke 9.12–17; John 6. 1–14.

Chapter 29: Paula Gooder

1 Houston Kraft, 2020, *Deep Kindness: A Revolutionary Guide for the Way we Think, Talk and Act in Kindness*, Simon Element: New York.
2 Paula Gooder, https://www.gooder.me.uk/, accessed 20.02.2026.
3 Luke 18.1–8.
4 Colossians 3.12.
5 Ephesians 4.32.
6 1 Corinthians 13.4.
7 Romans 2.4.
8 1 Corinthians 13.13.

Chapter 30: Andrew Rumsey

1 Houston Kraft, 2020, *Deep Kindness: A Revolutionary Guide for the Way We Think, Talk, and Act in Kindness*, Simon Element: New York, p. 135.

Chapter 31: Paul Northup

1 Greenbelt, https://www.greenbelt.org.uk/, accessed 20.02.2026.
2 Greenbelt, https://www.greenbelt.org.uk/greenbelt-festival/#the-greenbelt-manifesto, accessed 20.02.2026.

Chapter 32: David Porter

1 Coventry Cathedral, https://www.coventrycathedral.org.uk/reconciliation/reconciliation-ministry/litany-of-reconciliation, accessed 20.02.2026.

Chapter 33: Isabelle Hamley

1 Adam Philips and Barbara Taylor, 2010, *On Kindness*, Penguin: London.

Chapter 34: Chris Howson

1 Anne Frank, 1997, *A Diary of a Young Girl*, London: Penguin.
2 CLES – the Centre for Community Wealth Building defines anchor institutions as organizations which:
   1 Have an **important presence in a place**, usually through a combination of: being largescale employers, the largest purchasers of goods and services in the locality, controlling large areas of land and/or having relatively fixed assets.
   2 Are **tied to a particular place** by their mission, histories, physical assets and local relationships. Examples include local authorities, NHS trusts, universities, trade unions, large local businesses, the combined activities of the community and voluntary sector and housing associations.

   CLES, https://cles.org.uk/what-is-community-wealth-building/what-is-an-anchor-institution/, accessed 23.02.2026. I propose that a diocese and cathedral act as anchor institutions and as such play an important role in civic spaces and serve as secure foundational place-based organizations.

Chapter 35: Ayla Lepine

1 St James's Piccadilly, https://www.sjp.org.uk/whos-who/associate/, accessed 23.02.2026.
2 National Museums Liverpool, https://www.liverpoolmuseums.org.uk/walker-art-gallery, accessed 23.02.2026.
3 Art and Christianity, https://artandchristianity.org/, accessed 23.02.2026.
4 Janet Soskice, 2007, *The Kindness of God: Metaphor, gender, and religious language*, Oxford University Press: Oxford.
5 Galatians 5.22–23 describes the *fruit of the Spirit* as love, joy, peace, patience, kindness, goodness, faithfulness, gentleness, and self-control.
6 Collect at Evening Prayer, Book of Common Prayer.

Chapter 36: Steven Shakespeare

1 'Blessing for Lent – the seed of promise', from Steven Shakespeare, 2019, *The Earth Cries Glory: Daily prayer with creation*, Canterbury Press: Norwich, p. 29.
2 Liverpool Hope University, https://www.hope.ac.uk/, accessed 23.02.2026.

Chapter 37: Hannah Rich

1 Laura Jean Truman in Sarah Bessey (ed.), 2021, *A Rhythm of Prayer: A collection of meditations for renewal*, SPCK: London, pp. 73–4.
2 Christians on the Left, https://www.christiansontheleft.org.uk/, accessed 23.02.2026.
3 Theos, https://www.theosthinktank.co.uk/, accessed 23.02.2026.
4 Truman in Sarah Bessey, *Rhythm of Prayer*.
5 Church Urban Fund, https://cuf.org.uk/what-we-do/the-grace-project, accessed 23.02.2026.

Chapter 38: David Primrose

1 The Honey Foundation, https://www.honeyfoundation.org/, accessed 23.02.2026.

Chapter 39: Chine McDonald

1 Marcel Mauss, 2001, *The Gift: The form and reason for exchange in archaic societies*, Routledge: London.
2 Mauss, *The Gift*.
3 Bronisław Malinowski, 2022, *Argonauts of the Western Pacific*, Must Have Books: London.
4 Adam Philips and Barbara Taylor, 2010, *On Kindness*, Penguin: London.

Chapter 40: Year Five, St Cleopas C of E Primary School

1 St Cleopas CE Primary School, https://stcleopas.co.uk/, accessed 23.02.2026.
2 Show Racism the Red Card, https://www.theredcard.org/, accessed 23.02.2026.

Chapter 41: Rosemarie Mallett

1 Soft power is the ability to co-opt rather than coerce (in contrast to hard power).
2 Maryknoll Sisters, https://www.maryknollsisters.org/, accessed 23.02.2026.

Chapter 42: June Raymond

1 Jane Williams, 2018, *The Merciful Humility of God*, Bloomsbury: London, p. 56/7.
2 The Sisters of Notre Dame in Britain, https://www.snduk.org/, accessed 23.02.2026.
3 Julian of Norwich, 2015, *Revelations of Divine Love*, Oxford University Press: Oxford.
4 Carmen Bernos de Gasztold, 'The Prayer of the Dog', in *Prayers from the Ark*, trans. Rumer Godden, London: Macmillan, 1992.

Chapter 43: Michael Leyden

1 Jane Williams, 2018, *The Merciful Humility of God*, Bloomsbury: London, p. 143.
2 Emmanuel Theological College, https://emmanueltheologicalcollege.org.uk/, accessed 23.02.2026.
3 Stan van Hooft, 2013, *The Handbook of Virtue Ethics*, Routledge: London.
4 Galatians 5.22–23 describes the fruit of the Spirit as love, joy, peace, patience, kindness, goodness, faithfulness, gentleness, and self-control.
5 Gifts of the Holy Spirit such as wisdom, understanding, counsel, fortitude, knowledge, piety and fear of the Lord (1 Corinthians 12).

Chapter 44: Gill Morgan

1 Evangelical Alliance, https://www.eauk.org/news-and-views/celebrating-a-member ship-legacy, accessed 23.02.2026.
2 Ken is a massive Southampton FC supporter. The Dell was the name of their old ground.
3 Eugene Peterson, 2000, *Long Obedience in the Same Direction: Discipleship in an instant society*, Inter-Varsity Press: Downers Grove, IL.

Chapter 45: Azariah France-Williams

1 Azariah France-Williams, 2020, *Ghost Ship: Institutional Racism and the Church of England*, SCM Press.

Chapter 46: Stephen Cottrell

1 Stephen Cottrell, 2024, 'How we can remember the true spirit of Christmas', *The Yorkshire Post*, The Archbishop of York, https://www.archbishopofyork.org/news/latest-news/how-we-can-remember-true-spirit-christmas, accessed 23.02.2026.
2 Vatican News, https://www.vaticannews.va/en/pope/news/2025-10/sistine-chapel-ecumenical-prayer-service-with-pope-king-queen.html, accessed 23.02.2026.
3 'Love, joy, peace, patience, kindness, generosity, faithfulness, gentleness, and self-control' (Galatians 5.22–23).

Chapter 47: Molly Boot

1 Jane Austen, 2003, *Emma*, London: Penguin Classics.

Chapter 48: Steve Chalke

1 Richard Rohr, 2025, *The Tears of Things: Prophetic wisdom for an age of outrage*, SPCK: London, p. xxv.
2 Oasis, https://oasisuk.org/, accessed 23.02.2026.

Chapter 49: The Corbett Family

1 Martin Luther King Jr, 2017, *A Gift of Love: Sermons from strength to love*, Penguin Classics: London.
2 Craftivist Collective, https://www.craftivist-collective.com, accessed 23.02.2026.
3 Seen & Unseen, https://www.seenandunseen.com/contributors/henry-corbett, accessed 23.02.2026.
4 See also Rosemarie Mallet's reflection on soft power in Chapter 41.
5 Shrewsbury House, https://www.shrewsburyhouse.org.uk/everton-telegraph/, accessed 23.02.2026.
6 Matthew 10.16.
7 Martin Luther King.

Chapter 50: The students of St Margaret's C of E Academy

1 Matthieu Ricard, 2013, *Altruism: The science and psychology of kindness*, Atlantic Books: London, p. 691.

Chapter 51: James Green

1 Together Liverpool, https://togetherliverpool.org.uk/, accessed 23.02.2026.

Chapter 52: Mark Russell

1 The Children's Sopciety, https://www.childrenssociety.org.uk/about-us, accessed 23.02.2026.
2 Every Child Matters was an important government green paper published in 2003. It outlined the Government's proposals for the reform and improvement of childcare, following the death of Victoria Climbié and subsequent investigations by Lord Laming and various inspectorates dealing with children matters. Gov. UK, https://www.gov.uk/government/publications/every-child-matters, accessed 23.02.2026.
3 Cafod, https://cafod.org.uk/pray/catholic-social-teaching, accessed 23.02.2026.

Chapter 53: Steven Horne

1 Steven Horne, 2022, *Gypsies and Jesus: A Traveller theology*, Darton, Longman & Todd: London.
2 'Tapping out' is a wrestling term. It means a competitor verbally or physically signals surrender, resulting in an immediate loss. This is done by visibly tapping the mat, floor or opponent with a hand, or by verbally telling the referee. This action is

used to escape a submission hold that is causing pain or has the potential to cause injury.

Chapter 54: Adam Kelwick

1 Allah is Beautiful, and He loves beauty.
2 Inter Faith Week, https://www.interfaithweek.org/, accessed 23.02.2026.
3 Abdullah Quilliam Society, https://www.abdullahquilliam.org/, accessed 23.02.2026.
4 BBC News, https://www.bbc.co.uk/news/articles/cd194zkw4d90, accessed 23.02.2026.
5 Peace be upon you.

Chapter 55: Ariel Abel

1 El rachum: Compassionate God. The root word for *rachum* is *racham* (which is also means womb).

Chapter 56: Andi Oliver

1 R. J. Palacio, 2014, *Wonder*, Corgi: London.
2 Squash Liverpool, https://squashliverpool.co.uk/, accessed 23.02.2026.
3 Nena Cherry, 2025, *A Thousand Threads*, Vintage: London.

Chapter 57: Jane Williams

1 St Mellitus College, https://stmellitus.ac.uk/, accessed 23.02.2026.

Conclusion

1 C. S. Lewis, 1950, *The Lion the Witch and the Wardrobe*, 'Chapter 7: A day with the Beavers', Geoffrey Bles: London, p. 65.
2 Rutger Bregman, 2020, *Humankind: A hopeful history*, Bloomsbury: London, p. 4.
3 Frans De Waal, 2013, *The Bonobo and the Atheist: In search of humanism among the primates*, W. W. Norton & Company: New York, p. 43.
4 Rutger Bregman, 2020, *Humankind: A hopeful history*, Bloomsbury: London, p. 4.
5 Bregman, *Humankind*.
6 Bregman, *Humankind*.
7 Matthew 27.51; Mark 15.38; Luke 23.45.
8 Bregman, *Humankind*, p. 10.

www.ingramcontent.com/pod-product-compliance
Lightning Source LLC
LaVergne TN
LVHW041228150826
845673LV00005B/1323

* 9 7 8 1 7 8 6 2 2 7 4 0 9 *